Hotel Hell Beverly Hills and Beyond

*Stories Working
the Graveyard Shift*

Christie Smith

Robert D. Reed Publishers

Bandon, OR

Robert D. Reed Publishers
P.O. Box 1992
Bandon, OR 97411
Phone: 541-347-9882; Fax: -9883
E-mail: 4bobreed@msn.com
Website: www.rdrpublishers.com

Editor/Designer: Cleone Reed
Front cover: Implementation by Cleone Reed; Concept of a brick wall and fire by L Frank Manriquez, Native American artist, activist, and author

Soft Cover ISBN: 978-1-944297-34-3
eBook ISBN: 978-1-944297-35-0

Library of Congress Control Number: 2018907969

Designed and Formatted in the United States of America

Acknowledgments

First and foremost I thank God, my Lord and Savior, without which this book would have never happened. He has guided me through trials and tribulations and has given me the hope, help, and inspiration to follow my dreams.

I'd like to thank my family for always believing in me and always supporting me and always telling me that dreams really do come true. Mom Yvonne (Bonnie), Dad William (Bill), brothers David, Jeffrey, and Steven, and baby sister Jaimie. Steven and Jaimie are looking down on me from Heaven. My two children Randall (Randy) Smith and Alisha (Eesha) Ross, you are my rocks, the loves of my life, and my voices of reason.

I'd like to thank my cousin L. Frank Manriquez for taking my ideas about a book cover design and running with it and with her guidance and input made it into a true work of art. L. Frank has been an inspiration to me since I was a small child, and she first introduced me to the world of art both as an artist and as a spectator. She has always supported and lifted me up all of my life, and I was thrilled that she agreed to work on my book side by side.

I'd like to thank all of my colleagues—the list is too extensive to name you all—who worked with me over the years and never failed to jump in and support my plans of actions even when they didn't make a whole lot of sense at the time. I'd like to single out just a few: André Langston, Jennifer Lauren Butts, Sheldon Chun, and Momma Hen Elsie Gagarian. They were then and always will be the best crew that I ever worked with!

And finally a big thank you to Robert and Cleone Reed of Robert D. Reed Publishers for taking a chance on my baby and throughout the editing process shaped this rough gem into a diamond!

I hope you enjoy the read.

Christie

Contents

Introduction

The night auditor has the same basic function as a front desk or guest service agent except that they also prepare the "Books" for the accounting department the next morning. Night auditors usually function in a supervisory role in name only, not actually getting the official title or pay associated with a supervisor. Night auditors often work alone after midnight and oversee the PBX (telephone operators), bellmen, valet parking employees, room service attendants, and night housemen, even though those are not really departments that fall under the guise of the front desk. And they are working under a time deadline usually having to wrap up the entire night by no later than 2:30 a.m.

There is a lot happening in the middle of the night at a hotel of which most people are not aware. Night auditors do their utmost to pull it all off without a hitch, but sometimes disaster strikes! A prime example would be if there were a lot of late-night check-ins which would disrupt the attention to detail that is required for accounting purposes, or worse, the main computer crashes during the off-line process and we have to be on the phone with technical support in New York all night trying to figure out how to fix it! And believe me, those nights happen more often than anyone would think.

The graveyard shift can be very challenging, because as I stated before, the night auditors are usually flying solo. We don't get actual lunch breaks because there's no one to cover the front desk if we leave. So often times when we get a minute or two of down time, we wander off into the kitchen and rummage around for banquet leftovers or swipe a dish from the room service cart and bring it back to the front desk to chow down when we get a moment here or there. We can get pretty hungry about 2:00 a.m. The next opportunity to eat anything comes when we clock out at 7:00 a.m. Then we head out to the employee cafeteria for breakfast. And after a good breakfast, that's usually when we hit our "Wall" and total exhaustion sets in as we start to relax and let go of all the stress and tension of the previous night. Driving home gets tricky because we are fighting off sleep trying to get home in one piece.

The stories in this book are culled from my 20-some odd years of working as a front desk agent and as a night auditor in four-star hotels in and around the Los Angeles area. A front desk agent's basic function is to greet hotel guests upon their arrival at the hotel and check them into their respective rooms. The front desk agents are basically there to ensure that their guests have an absolutely outstanding visit to their establishment, with the final goal being that they will tell people positive reports and bring years of repeat business.

In the following pages I intend to regale you with all kinds of interesting tales of the crazy and unbelievable situations that the night auditor comes across. It's never the same story ever. And I'm sure it will be very eye-opening to you as prospective and former guests. It'll make you want to ask more in-depth questions when you check into a hotel in the future, and you'll probably be a lot more critical and suspicious about the state of your hotel rooms! It's not my intention to make you feel this way; it's just a by-product of the stories, and it's human nature at its best and sometimes worst. You'll probably thank me later.

Chapter 1: Bodies and Bits

The East Wing

I was hired at my first hotel at the tender young age of 23. The hotel, now defunct and demolished to make way for condominiums and retail space, was near my house; and it had been a pretty prominent fixture in my neighborhood for many years. It consisted of a twelve-story tower and four separate two-story wings, and there were about 400 rooms in all.

I was just a fledgling desk agent and had barely been on the job for a month when I had checked in an older married couple while on one of my first graveyard shifts. They checked in at a little past 11:00 p.m. and went promptly up to their room. The next morning as I was preparing to leave, that same older married couple caught me at the desk and wanted to talk to me about the night that they had. It seems there was an awful smell in their room, and it made sleeping somewhat uncomfortable because they couldn't identify where the smell was coming from. I apologized for their inconvenience and offered to send housekeeping up to their room to check it out.

Housekeeping said that there was indeed an odor there, but they felt that they had handled the situation with air freshener. I caught the couple again the next night when they had returned to the hotel from a day of sightseeing and fine dining. They asked me about their room, and I assured them that the smell was gone; so they went up and went to bed.

Okay, the next morning, this would have been their second night stay, I again caught the couple at around 7:00 a.m. They had approached me and again stated that the smell had actually gotten worse since housekeeping had been in there. I felt so bad, apologized to the couple for their inconvenience, and insisted that I give them a new room, in a different building. I even upgraded them to poolside for no extra charge. I also offered a free meal in our restaurant. The couple said that all that fuss was not necessary, but that they were happy that I was easily willing to make things right for them. So I issued them new room keys and sent them along their way.

As soon as they were out of sight I picked up the phone and called housekeeping and I said "Someone get up to that damn room and find that smell!" I then clocked out and went home.

When I arrived back at the hotel to start my shift that night at 11:00 p.m., I noticed some unusual activity in the east wing. More specifically, there was police activity as the whole east wing was cordoned off with police tape! I curiously asked the departing swing shift what was happening. One of the desk agents went on to explain that housekeeping had been up to the room with the bad smell and that it was an awful, wretched, disgusting smell that made one want to gag and vomit.

Housekeeping began systematically taking the room apart— first the curtains, then the waste baskets, and then furniture. They also stripped the bed sheets off and shampooed the carpet, and they still couldn't find the source of the smell. The last place to look was in between the mattress and box spring. Maybe there was mold? We were quite close to the ocean and mold can get to be a big problem.

When the housekeeping crew pulled the mattress off of the bed… there inside an upside down box spring was the dead body of a woman! We later learned that it was a local prostitute, and LAPD (Los Angeles Police Department) detectives had been processing the scene all day. I was mortified beyond all mortification! I felt so bad that I had made that older couple sleep on top of a dead body for two nights! If the LAPD detectives had any information about the dead hooker or who might have killed her, well they weren't talking to anyone at the hotel. To my honest recollection, we never did find out the whole story. And the east wing was closed up tight for over a month!

A Room with a View

I know this is going to sound rather macabre, but suicidal guests often book hotel rooms for the soul purpose of ending their lives in them. I guess if they're lonely and don't have any family or friends, they are afraid that no one will find their bodies before they start to decompose. Or maybe they don't want to make a mess at their own places. Or maybe they want to live it up one last night in a four-star hotel before their big send off. Whatever it is, their excuses run the gamut.

Who knows why they do it? And they don't always leave a suicide note either. Believe it or not, a big hotel, one with 500 or more rooms, gets an average of two to three dead bodies per month. Some are from natural causes, such as a heart attack, stroke, or old age. Some are from accidental drug or alcohol overdoses, and some are actually from being the victim of a homicide or some other violence. And some are from suicide. The worst ones are the self-inflicted gun shots. Those are always messy, and they always severely traumatize the housekeeping staff when they inadvertently find them after they knock on the door and there is no answer and they let themselves in.

In those cases, especially, the hotel has to do what is called a "deep clean," meaning the whole entire room has to be stripped down to the wall studs. The carpet, ceiling, and drywall all has to come out and be replaced with brand new drywall; and of course all the furniture has to come out and be sanitized before it goes into the dumpster. The room is usually "Out of order" for weeks, even after everything has been replaced. Why? Because as hokey as it sounds, the staff of hotels are worried about residual spirit activity that might take place in a room because a person was in a state of unrest when they offed themselves. Yes, hotels can be haunted! But you'll rarely hear them admit to such a thing. They fear bad PR and busloads of amateur ghost hunters wanting to stay the night in one of those rooms. Some hotels actually go with it and market themselves as a haunted hotel, especially if one of the dead guests was a celebrity.

Medical Maladies

Being one block away from a major Hospital and Trauma Center does have its perks for certain guests of both the hospital and the hotel. When a guest suddenly fell ill, it was just a short jaunt to the Emergency Room; and in some incidents doctors even made house calls since we were so close by. Sometimes patients who had minor elective surgery came to our hotel to recuperate so that if any complications should arise they could get help fast. Celebrities that have procedures done at the hospital and don't want the infamous Paparazzi hanging around also came to our hotel to convalesce in relative privacy. Either way, it was a win-win for both the hospital and the hotel. Except for the time we got this next guest that I'm about to tell you about.

A woman I'd say looked to be in her early 40's was discharged as a patient from the hospital but still needed to be close by for ongoing treatments. She walked a little funny and was clothed literally from head to toe: baggy pants, knee-hi socks with sandals, long sleeves, gloves covering her hands, a neck scarf, a head scarf, and a pair of dark sunglasses. It struck me as odd since we were in the middle of summer in Los Angeles and the temperature outside was a balmy 79 degrees. When she came in, she did not have a reservation but was told by the hospital staff that there was a specially negotiated rate for hospital patients. She showed us her hospital discharge papers as proof that she had been a patient. We asked her how long she would be staying. She said she didn't know because her treatment was ongoing. As we were conducting our business, I became aware of a foul stench in the

14

air. It wasn't the normal bodily odor of say B.O. or someone passing gas or bad breath, but it was a pretty rank and funky smell, and it seemed to be coming from this woman. She hurriedly signed her registration card and collected her room keys and went upstairs to her room. She had initially stated that she wanted seven days but that she had expected to extend her stay.

Her first few days went off without a hitch, and each day she would call down to housekeeping and ask them NOT to service her room. Now a guest can certainly request that housekeeping not service their room for a few days, but anything more than that and they get antsy. They want to know why a person would not want their room serviced. Believe it or not, there are some guests that actually bring their own bedsheets, blankets, and pillows to hotels because they're either germaphobes or they feel better sleeping on their own sheets. This was not the case for this particular guest.

On about day four, other guests on her floor were starting to complain about the strong stench in the hallway of their floor. She ordered room service for every meal and would leave the empty trays outside of her door each time. The smell was so bad that housekeeping demanded to be let in to clean her room. The housekeeping manager went to her door, and when she opened the door the housekeeping manager could see that this poor woman had some sort of extreme type of skin psoriasis all over her body, and her skin was sloughing off, and that's where the strong odor was coming from. She said she was seeking treatment at the hospital, but she never left her room and no medical personnel ever came to call on her. She also left dirty towels outside of her door and asked for clean towels every day. Now that housekeeping knew what they were dealing with, they put special protocols in place to protect our employees because we didn't know if what she had was contagious.

Two weeks went by, and when she called to extend her stay for another week we told her no. The entire floor that she was staying on smelled awful. And as a result we couldn't put any other guests on her floor and that was bad for business. There was some back and forth between the management and her as they tried to get her to leave or let housekeeping in. What we had to do in essence was to serve her with a legal eviction notice. Her credit card was still good so nonpayment wasn't the issue. She was really upset and fired up when she received that eviction notice. She was up in arms and threatening legal action against the hotel.

Eventually we won the eviction in court and then called the Los Angeles Sheriff's Department to come out and forcibly remove the woman from her room. They wore medical face masks and latex gloves when they retrieved her. She was screaming and yelling all the way down the elevator and all through the lobby and even yelled a few choice expletives to the valet parking attendant. The woman drove off and we never saw her again.

But now we had an even bigger problem—her room! We ended up having to do a "deep clean." Her room was totally stripped down to the wall studs; and the drywall, carpet, and furniture all had to come out and be destroyed and disposed of properly and safely. Every towel that was outside of her room was burned in the hotels incinerator, and every room service tray was bleached. We even had to replace the carpet in the entire hallway and repaint the entire floor to get rid of the smell. It was a nightmarish situation, and I know I'll always feel uneasy before lying down in a hotel bed for the rest of my life.

Housekeeping Horrors

We've all seen those news stories about hotel housekeeping horror stories. The "60 minutes" and "20/20" television news shows often take black lights into hotel rooms and show all the leftover DNA and other bacteria and germs that are present on the bed sheets, comforters, and carpets. But does it actually happen at a four-star hotel? The answer is: yes it does! The following is a nightly report from the night audit.

First, the guest in room 921 commented that on his last stay the room attendant asked him if he would like clean towels.

16

He declined the towels but said that he would like to have clean glasses. The room attendant took a dirty rag from off of her cart and cleaned the glasses with soap and water in his bathroom sink and used another dirty rag to dry the glasses and left them for the guest. The guest expressed concern about the way in which his request was handled. He thought it was rather inappropriate for this caliber of a hotel and he won't be drinking out of our in-room glasses again.

Second, the guest in room 837 checked in and completely unpacked and crawled into bed and was horrified to find that the mattress was soaking wet! It wasn't the sheets or the comforters; she pulled them off and exposed the mattress and found the mattress wet. She travels for a living and this has never happened to her ever! I immediately sent Bellman Francis to move her to another room and offered her breakfast coupons and drink coupons for the remaining three days of her stay.

Third, the minibar in room 305 has not been serviced for at least three days and the minibar slip that the guest fills out was still inside the minibar. The minibar attendant charged the guest on that day but never removed the trash and debris from the minibar. Later a different minibar attendant, seeing the blue slip, assumed that the guest had not been charged and reposted the charge thus overcharging the guest, which later had to be adjusted off of the guest's bill showing a loss of revenue. The minibar attendants must be more consistent in rendering their service.

Additionally many of the minibars have broken locks, and we at the front desk do not know which rooms have broken locks so it's impossible to know what "cash" customers to put into a room, which more often than not results in the "cash" guest taking the entire contents of the minibar without paying for it. The guest simply puts out the "Do not disturb" sign on their doorknob so that the minibar will not be checked until after the "cash" guest has checked out of their room. FIX THE DAMN MINIBARS!!! We received a one-million-dollar facelift to the exterior of the hotel; how about a little attention to the inside???

Fourth, there seems to be some confusion with the room service late-night menus 11 p.m. to 5:30 a.m. Some menus are incorrectly showing a menu item that we no longer have. Many guests have been sorely disappointed when they are told that they cannot order that item at the times that are indicated on the menu. Can we please have someone check the menus and get the correct menus in place as soon as possible? We don't really want to have to make adjustments unnecessarily because of confusion or misrepresentation on behalf of our establishment.

In closing I hope that these issues can be resolved quickly and adequately, both for the benefit of our staff and our valued guests. Take pride in your hotel!

Pain Killer

Neil the bellman says to Sheldon the night auditor "The lady in 732 wants some aspirin but the gift shop is already closed and she doesn't want to walk across the street to the drug store; what should I do?"

Sheldon replies, "Go downstairs to the employee locker rooms. In the hallway there is a machine that dispenses little packets of aspirin for 50 cents. Go get two packs and then charge her $1.00 a piece."

Frat Party

One summer night there was a rather large function going on in the main banquet room. It was a local fraternity from one of the colleges in the area. I won't say which fraternity so as not to ruffle any feathers. The party was raging; the DJ that they had hired had everyone in the place jumping. Usually as the night draws nearer to 2 a.m., the banquet staff tries to slowly wrap up the evening and get everyone moving on home. So this night was no different in that regard. About 1:15 a.m., a small group of frat boys grabbed a cab and went on a liquor run so that they could continue the party into the wee hours of the morning. The fraternity had reserved several rooms in the hotel just on the off chance that someone would be too hammered to make it home. I saw the group come back through the lobby at 1:55 a.m., just under the 2 a.m. limit for purchasing alcohol in the state of California. Several of the boys had cases of beer in their hands as they made their way up to their rooms. At 2 a.m. the banquet was officially shut down, the cleanup began, and a big group of boys went up to their rooms.

As one would guess, there were several noise complaints from other guests that were trying to sleep in nearby rooms. But *boys will be boys*, as they say. The hotel security went up there a few times and eventually got the boys to settle down. And the rest of the night was uneventful.

Skip to the next day. The boys, obviously hung over from the night before, began filing out a few at a time. The surprise was for housekeeping that morning as they entered the boys' now vacant room; it was a disaster area! They said it looked like one Hell of a party had taken place. The housekeeper's likened it to an F5 tornado. The room was literally ransacked—empty beer cans and bottles everywhere, bed linens on the floor, and towels thrown around. There was a strong stench of urine on the mattresses, vomit on the floor next to a bed, and used condoms spread out randomly across the room. Those boys did more damage to the room than what they had paid for.

When something of this nature occurs, the room must be put "Out of Order" and a "deep clean" is ordered, which puts the room out of order for up to fourteen days while engineering crews go in to replace the carpeting; and sometimes the drywall has to removed and replaced as well. Then a fresh coat of paint and new factory-sealed furniture and bedding is put in, so the room can be put back on line.

Obviously things like this happen in hotels and they can't always control it or stop it. They just have to deal with the aftermath.

Hanky Panky

People rent hotel rooms for a myriad of reasons, and generally people don't come right out and tell you why they're there or what they plan on doing in the room. Generally people will tell you that they're on vacation or on a business trip. Beyond those reasons, the hotel staff doesn't know anything until after a guest checks out and housekeeping gets the first look at the aftermath. Staff does see people bringing unusual items through the lobby on their way to their rooms. I've seen people try to smuggle in animals, bulky car parts, extra people, and other items that I really can't describe or explain. That being said, the next guest that I'm going to tell you about was one for the record books!

The guest, I'll just call him Mr. Johnson (you'll see why in a minute), checked in to a suite for a three-day stay. There didn't seem to be anything odd or unusual about Mr. Johnson, and the check in went just fine. He was checking in by himself and said that no one else would be occupying the room; but he did ask where the hotel freight elevators were, and he asked to be put onto a floor that was less occupied than the others. After Mr. Johnson got settled in his room, a moving van pulled up into the valet parking area, opened the doors, and began unloading all kinds of equipment onto rolling carts and headed for the freight elevators! I asked them where they were going, and they indicated that they were headed up to Mr. Johnson's room! There were at least six guys bringing in this equipment, and they made several trips until the van was empty. Then they drove the van around the corner and parked it on a side street. Of course I was curious, so I asked, "Just exactly what IS all this equipment?"

The guys said that it was film equipment, lights, cameras, sound equipment, etc.

So I asked, "Why is all this camera equipment going up to Mr. Johnson's room?" There was a guy with a lanyard around his neck with a card that read some kind of film production company's name on it, and he said that he was the director and that they would be filming an adult movie for the next couple of days! In other words they were shooting a porno!

Well, to my knowledge you have to have city permits to film on location, and secondly, you have to have the hotel's permission before you bring in any film crew for any reason. There are also insurance issues to work out, not to mention the inconvenience to the other paying guests and the general disgust guests would feel if they were aware that there was an adult film crew next to their room. Also, the hotel's reputation would get "Hit" because now they'd be forever known as a sleazy establishment that lets these types of things happen.

I was at a loss as to what to do about this situation. It's certainly NOT in the employee handbook! I called hotel security and asked if there was protocol in place for this kind of thing, and he said no. I called the LAPD to ask what if anything could be done, but they didn't seem to have an answer other than that they could send an officer to issue them a citation for their lack of proper permits, but then again they weren't code-enforcement agents.

So what could I do? I just made sure that no other guests that night were given rooms on that floor. I spoke to the film director and asked him to keep his filming as low key as possible and to expect a visit from hotel management in the morning. He thanked me and said that he would keep the disturbance to a minimum. As far as I know, the next day the film crew was asked to leave the hotel because the room was showing "Vacant" in the system that night when I came back on duty.

"People will forget what you said.
They will forget what you did.
But they will never forget
how you made them feel."

~ Maya Angelou

Chapter 2: Celebrity Stories

Hefner's Heifers

It was pretty late one Saturday summer night in Los Angeles. It was just a tad past 2 a.m. when several long black limousines pulled into the valet parking area, and suddenly the lobby started to fill up with beautiful, buxom babes! They all looked like they could be super models rivaling the best of the best. It wasn't such an odd occurrence getting a late-night crowd after a party breaks up. What was odd about these particular girls was the fact that all they were wearing was six-inch stilettos and barely-there lingerie. All of them were scantily clad. It was just a bit chilly outside, and none of the ladies had overcoats nor pocketbooks.

Well, curiosity got the best of me, so I walked out from behind the front desk and waltzed over to the girls and asked one of them, "Why are all of you in nothing but lingerie?"

One of the girls laughed and explained to me that they had all been to a party at the world famous Playboy Mansion and that they had all been personally invited by Hugh Hefner himself. They all said that they were centerfold hopefuls.

I've got to admit that I felt just a tiny bit intimidated by both their beauty and their courage in pursuit of such a lofty prize. After the last limousine had pulled in and delivered its cargo, a couple of rather large framed men in three-piece suits came in to personally escort each and every woman up to her room. I myself had a fantasy about posing for Playboy Magazine, and it was awesome to actually meet women who had "Gone for it!" Girls like them keep girls like me hopeful and optimistic.

Surrounding myself with beautiful women
keeps me young.

~ Hugh Hefner

Gary's Dilemma

One fall night while I was on duty, actually I had just arrived for the start of my shift at 11 p.m., I checked in a few late arrivals and sent them on their way; but as I was checking in the last reservation slated for that evening, I noticed a very small black man, who actually looked more like a child, walk into the lobby. Upon closer examination I realized that Gary Coleman had just walked into my lobby! Gary was the child star of the sitcom "Different Strokes," a show that I used to watch religiously as a youngster. The show ran from 1978 thru 1986, and it had a pretty good run and even touted a few spin offs... a fun thing to "Google."

Anyhow, Gary approached the front desk and asked what the rate was for a possible one-week stay. Since he had no reservations and didn't qualify for any discounts, I had to quote him the rack rate, which is ultimately the highest rate possible in the hotel with the only exception being suites, which are obviously much, much higher. Gary said that was fine. I gave him a registration card to fill out and then I ran his credit card, but I noticed that the address that Gary had listed was a condominium complex three blocks away on Green Valley Circle. So I innocently asked him why he needed a hotel room when he only

24

lived down the street. It just seemed odd to me. Gary laughed and said that his maid had up and quit the week before and that now his condo was so dirty that he didn't feel comfortable staying there. He said it would probably take about a week or so to hire a new maid, so until then he would be staying with us. The last thing Gary asked for before he left the front desk was for a napkin and a straw. I said, "Sure, not a problem," and I walked over to the hotel bar and got him one straw and one napkin.

The following day I was grocery shopping and at the checkout counter I noticed a headline, and I'm paraphrasing here, "Poor Gary rejected by the girl in the train store." As a matter of fact, Gary's quest for finding love with the girl that didn't want him had been playing out in the tabloids for weeks; and Gary was feeling lonely, embarrassed, and rejected.

On the second night of his stay, Gary popped into the lobby around midnight and struck up a light-hearted conversation with me. It was mostly just small talk about anything and everything, and I was feeling pretty excited that I was actually making friends with a real-life celebrity. He hung out with me for about an hour, and then he again asked for a single napkin and one straw.

On the third night Gary called the front desk at about 11:30 p.m. I caught the call and he asked me if it would be okay for him to come down to the lobby and chat for a few. I said, "Sure Mr. Coleman; I'm not too terribly busy at the moment." So about ten minutes later he arrived in the lobby. He looked around and found a stack of free local papers, picked up a copy of "LA Weekly," and began perusing the "Personals" section. He laughed and said that he had just seen a real funny ad in the "Women seeking Men" section, so he read it out loud so I could hear it. We both laughed hysterically and that prompted Gary to keep reading. The more he read, the more unique, interesting, and funnier they got. Gary read for about ten minutes and said that he thought he might actually answer one of those ads. Then he put the paper back on the rack, turned around, and walked up to me and point blank asked me to go out with him! He said that I was beautiful, smart, and funny; and we had already found that we had several things in common, so why not? I'll admit that I was totally caught off guard by Gary. I smiled at him and told him that it was against hotel policy to date or fraternize with guests. I could actually get fired for that. But I did thank him for his flattery. Gary then asked for his one napkin and one straw again and asked me to just think about it.

I went home the next morning and told my family about my encounter with Gary Coleman, and they were pretty curious about what my answer to Gary might be. I thought about it for a while and then glanced at my copy of "The National Enquirer" on my coffee table and thought to myself, *Oh Hell no! I could just picture the photograph of Gary and me out on a date and the headline that read "Who is Gary Coleman's new mystery woman?" or "Gary proposes to mystery woman."* So aside from losing my job, my face would be plastered all over the world!

It got to be a nightly routine of Gary coming down to the lobby and talking with me at the start of my shift. He was a great guy! Lighthearted, funny, intelligent, and of course handsome. He kept asking me to go out with him, but aside from the fact that I could be in serious trouble at work and be made infamous in the tabloids, I had a boyfriend at the time and I was raising my infant daughter to boot. I did let Gary down easy because I knew what he was going through. I gave him dating advice, and I told him that things would work out for the best eventually and that he just had to be patient. "The right girl is going to come along when you least expect it."

And every night he would ask for a single napkin and a straw?

Day 7 finally rolled around and Gary was due to check out. That night he told me that he had finally found a new maid, and she said that his place was all nice and clean and he could come back anytime. So, alas, he was on his way. But I was still very curious about one thing? Why did he need a napkin and a straw every night? So I asked him about it? He laughed and said he didn't want to go into detail about it. He thanked me for making his stay with us amazing. He said that he'd never forget me. Gary passed away in May 2010, and it was a bit of a shocker, and in the end he was able to finally find true love. Rest in Peace, Mr. Coleman, and I'll certainly never forget you!

Randy Travis

The country crooner Randy Travis was rumored to be in the hotel one night; and as I was such a big fan of country music, I just had to confirm that fact. I looked through the alphabetical list of guests, and I couldn't find his name anywhere. So I was just a little disappointed until I saw Randy Travis actually walking through my lobby! He was checking out, and the reason I couldn't find him was that he had stayed under his wife's maiden name; and at that time he was still married to Elizabeth Hatcher. Randy got to the front door and then abruptly turned around and made a b-line straight for me! He walked up to my station and handed me a $50 bill and said, "Pardon me miss; can you make change for this?"

I was so star struck! I maintained my professional composure and made change of two $20's and a $10, and he thanked me and walked off into the sunset as it were. I kept that $50 bill in my work bank for months afterward, only because Randy Travis had touched it. Silly sounding, I know, but it was all I had to hang onto to represent a great moment in time.

A lot of celebrities stayed in our hotels under assumed names, and we never knew that they were in the hotel unless or until we happened to get a glance at them while they were walking through the lobby or were checking in or out.

There is a strict policy of not asking for autographs or photo ops, but that didn't always stop the employees from trying if they felt that it was an appropriate time or wouldn't bother or inconvenience a celebrity. Most celebrities were glad to cooperate in those instances, and we could usually get a quick autograph or picture when nobody was looking.

Bo Diddley

The legendary R & B musician Bo Diddley was checking out one morning. It was very busy and the checkout lines were eight and ten people deep at all the stations. I didn't know that it was Bo at first because he was at the back of one of the lines. He was wearing a little wide-brimmed black bowler hat that had his name embroidered in silver sequins on the front. All I could see was this little black hat that was jumping from one line to the other looking for the fastest line. I figured this guest was in a hurry, so I decided to jump out of my area and slip off to the side and call him over. When I finally saw him, his face was unmistakable; it was Bo Diddley in the flesh. I said "Hey there, Mr. Bo, you look like you're in some kind of a hurry."

He said he was and he wanted to let me know that he had been playing around with the remote control on the TV, and he thought that he might have accidentally ordered a movie that naturally he did not watch. I said "That won't be a problem." I noticed that the movie was a comedy and that I had seen it in the theater recently, so I gave him my impromptu movie review.

After I made the adjustment on his account, it was the policy of the hotel to note the adjustment on a little slip of green paper about the size of a Post-it Note pad and file it with the rest of the paperwork. I printed up his receipt and asked him to sign it, and then very quickly and stealthily I pulled off a piece of the green adjustment slip and flipped it upside down and asked him to sign that as well. Sneaky I know.

28

Now Bo started up a little conversation with me and complimented my looks and my professionalism; and he asked me if I'd like to meet his Bass player, who was his nephew and who was a nice boy that needed a girlfriend. He really tried hard to sell me on him, and he kept waving his nephew over but the nephew never came over. We laughed about it, and when Bo had left the hotel I had a chance to get a really good look at the autograph. It said "To Christie, rock and roll 2000, Bo Diddley." He was awesome! Bo Diddley passed in June 2008, Rest in Peace and keep rocking in Heaven.

I thank you in advance for the great round of applause I'm about to get.

~ Bo Diddley

Muhammad Ali

One afternoon I was doing a rare thing and covering for one of the swing-shift girls that had called out sick that day and found myself on the 3 p.m. to 11 p.m. shift. It was about 4 p.m. or 5 p.m. when I spotted what looked like "The Greatest!" And it was! It was Muhammad Ali in person walking through my lobby! I almost couldn't contain my excitement at seeing him. I had watched almost every one of his professional fights, and I knew his stats and he was the greatest! He had by his side a personal valet who was escorting him through the lobby. Ali walked about halfway through the lobby and then sat down in the most visible area he could find. His valet and he sat there for hours, and people were stopping to say hello to the champ.

When I got a ten-minute break, I also walked out to meet my hero. I asked him why he was sitting out here for so long, but his speech had been so profoundly affected by his advanced Parkinson's disease that he really couldn't talk His valet answered for him. He said that Ali just wants to be with his fans. And that just melted my heart. I thought, *Now here is a true hero, a man of the people, a kind and caring man. Wow.* A few other employees came down to talk to the champ and get an autograph which, bless his heart, he tried to sign, but his motor functions were not all that great anymore either. I just remembered how good he looked. Like when he was in his prime! He was still larger than life, and he would always be my hero. Muhammad Ali died in June of 2016. Rest in Peace, Champ.

Don't count the days; make the days count.

~ Muhammad Ali

Xzibit

One night I was manning the front desk when this young man walked into the lobby and wandered around a bit. I wasn't sure if he was lost or waiting for friends. After about ten minutes, he approached the front desk, and I asked him if he had a reservation.

He said that yes he did.

So I asked him for his name and he said "Xzibit" and I was instantly confused. I said "Eggs who?"

And again he said "Xzibit" so I innocently asked, "Well how do you spell that?" I didn't know exactly who he was—a prominent rapper and TV host of the show, "Pimp my ride." So he spelled it out for me "X-Z-I-B-I-T."

I looked through the list of arrivals, and sure enough the name Xzibit was there. I asked him if that was his first or last name and he said, "It's just Xzibit." I had him fill out a registration card and saw that his room was being "Direct billed" and his record company was picking up the tab, so there was no need to take his credit card but I did get a signature. He was very kind and completely professional, and I love guests like that. I still didn't know who he was, but obviously he was somebody.

I went home the next morning and asked my two teenage kids if they knew who Xzibit was.

They got so excited and wanted to know everything! They said, "Mom, do you know who that is?"

I said "No, I don't," and laughed. Of all the celebrities that I have encountered at work, Xzibit was the one guy that they were most impressed by. Man, do I have a cool job!

Never define your success by somebody else's success. I never looked at another man's grass to tell how green mine should be.

~ Xzibit

The Proposal

This particular hotel had a number of high-profile guests staying there, and when I say high profile, I mean professional athletes—mostly NBA players that are in transition from one team to another and are either looking for permanent housing or are waiting for the season to end before moving on to their new teams.

One LA Clipper in particular, I won't divulge his name, had been in our hotel for several months already. He was resistant to finding permanent housing because he said that he didn't really like California and especially didn't like Los Angeles. He was pretty much a night owl like myself; and two or three nights a week, he would come down to the lobby around 3 a.m. and would just want to talk. At that time of the night, the mainframe of the computer was off-line doing the "One Button," and nobody was obviously checking in or out at that time. So, yes, I had some time to kill. We would talk for an hour or so about a lot of different things, like growing up as a kid and wondering what kind of a job we would have when we grew up. We talked about our families, the crazy aunts and uncles; we talked about our adventures and what we still would like to accomplish in this life. He was a great guy—6 feet 6 inches of African American basketball-ball-playing energy. And he was very handsome as well. I'm sure he had plenty of girls chasing him.

One particular night he came down to the lobby at his usual time, but I could tell that he definitely had something on his mind. He seemed almost distraught. I said, "Hey big fella, what's up? What's on your mind?"

He informed me that he was notified just that morning that he was being traded to the Washington Bullets, and he wasn't at all happy about it. He hated Seattle more than he hated Los Angeles. He couldn't understand how this could be happening to him, and he was trying to figure a way out. He then turned to me and just asked me, "Will you marry me?"

I had to catch my breath for a moment, and then he asked me again, "Come on; marry me!"

To which I replied "You barely even know me. We've never been on a date; you don't know what I'm like to live with. I'm white and have two small children. You're black and rich and famous. Why on earth would you want to marry me?"

He said, "I know enough about you to know that we would be great together, and I would treat you like a Queen. I'll take you to see the world." He continued, "I've decided not to go to Seattle. I'm going to go to Italy and join a professional team there."

I said, "But you can have your choice of any woman; you can have a super model, for God sakes." I asked "Why me?"

He simply said, "I can take you home to Mother. All those other girls are fake and are just after my money. They want to be trophy wives."

I said, "Well, this is an awful lot to put on a girl you hardly know. I have to have a few days to think this over."

He said, "You've got three days, and then I'm gone out of your life forever."

I'll admit that I was in definite freak-out mode. After all, I had two small children and was currently in a relationship, although not a great relationship, but I was still trying to make it work. I ultimately got way too scared of the unknown and turned him down. Italy was a continent away from my family and friends, so no, I just couldn't, or should I say, I just wouldn't, jeopardize that. I know that I probably made the worst decision of my life turning down his proposal, but hey, what did I know about life's uncertainties and financial hardships? I was just a 24-year-old kid. Staying true to his word, he left three days later, and I never saw nor heard from him ever again. Que sera sera.

The Klingon Invasion

Now I'm a pretty big *Star Trek* fan of the original series starring William Shatner and Leonard Nimoy. So I was naturally excited when I learned that there was a Star Trek Convention coming to my hotel. I couldn't get tickets myself to the event, but I was just happy to be a spectator at work. I knew I'd probably see some way-out stuff. Sure enough, there were all kinds of alien lifeforms traipsing through the lobby that weekend. The only downside was that I never actually got a glimpse of Captain Kirk or Spock. I guess they were in super stealth mode. They must have had the Enterprise beam them back up every night.

What I did get to see, however, was a couple of real-life Klingon Warriors. Their makeup was amazing, and their homemade costumes looked like they were authentically pulled from the wardrobe of the original TV series. The two rather rough Klingons approached me at the front desk and were asking some mundane questions about sightseeing tours of Los Angeles and where the best eateries in town were. But something was just different about these two Klingons. Something was drawing me in, and somehow the Alpha Klingon asked me out, to which I had readily accepted. He said, "Great! Why don't you come up to my room later and watch me take off my makeup before we leave?" I knew it was risky going up to his room, but I was already on the hook.

I learned when I went up to his room that night that he was a medically retired Los Angeles Police K-9 cop. His name was Dave. He explained that at age 32, he had a heart attack while he was on duty. He blamed it on the extreme daily stress of the job. He showed me his badge and his shoulder patch, and he even had his K-9 companions picture ID in his wallet.

I was fresh out of a relationship and fresh out of a multimillion dollar proposal, so I figured that I had nothing to lose by going out with Dave. It was a nice dinner with him and his brother. The next day Dave came down to the lobby on his way to the festivities, and he stopped to teach me a Klingon word, "Hadiback" (Ha-dee-Bach). In Klingon, it is a sign of respect to call someone a Hadiback; or in other words, you're calling someone an "Animal." He also told me his Klingon name was Lt. Ta-corg-tie-bac-Tur-as, and his brother was Ta-creed-tie-bac The-as. I'm actually amazed that I even remember that since it's such a specialized and obscure alien name. Anyhow, there was time for one last photo op with my two favorite aliens before they had to head back to Tulare, California, Dave's retirement home. He was too stressed out in Los Angeles and opted for a small-town lifestyle.

So just remember, if you ever find yourself staring down a big scary Klingon, immediately call him or her a Hadiback and it might just save your life!

After all, it's pretty hard to be prejudiced against blacks and gays when you're a-okay with Klingons and the Green Men of Mars.

~ Lou Anders

No Pay

Occasionally the hotel will get a guest that makes a fuss and then tries every angle to get out of paying their bill. Those kinds of guests are looking for what we refer to as comps. Initially, the front desk agent has been empowered to resolve guest disputes and keep the costs or loss to the hotel to a minimum. The higher up in the chain of command the guest has to go to have things resolved, the more money it's going to cost the hotel. So say a small dispute over a $10 phone bill that can easily be resolved at the front desk by merely adjusting the guest's bill could potentially run into the hundreds of dollars in comps if it has to go all the way to corporate headquarters to be resolved.

There are a lot of disputes with the guests, most of which are minor, such as being charged for a phone call that wasn't made or overcharged for a local call, or a minibar charge when the guest didn't take anything from the minibar, etc. Then there are the more difficult complaints, such as problems with the food in room service or the restaurant, lost reservations, the guest room not being serviced, or noisy neighbors. Finally the really big problems include things such as guest injury, valet parking damaging a vehicle, granting a person access to a guest room without asking for a proper identification, stealing from a guest room, or offering drugs or prostitutes to a guest. The latter of these is obviously really, really bad; and unfortunately, these things occur in hotels throughout the world on a daily basis

Now the exceptions are true jewels and rarities in the hotels. They are always unique and disturbing. One that sticks out in my memory and never seems to fade away and is always entertaining and unbelievable to me is the ploys of Mr. A.

Mr. A was some sort of famous journalist in Italy. He stayed with us over the course of ten days during the Oscar celebrations so that he could interview celebrities and attend parties and send all the good gossip back to Italy. Some of the Italian employees that worked in the hotel knew of him and were also aware of his reputation for being rude and difficult with everyone. Needless to say, they weren't impressed by any of this.

Mr. A and his traveling associates went into the gift shop every morning and harassed the cashier about her lack of Italian merchandise and complained about their specially ordered Italian newspaper.

They were on the Penthouse floor and everyday would leave cardboard boxes and packing materials strewn throughout the hallways as if the hallway was the city dump.

On Mr. A's final two nights, he called the front desk to complain that he was woken from his restful slumber by a low-flying helicopter at 6 a.m. in the morning. There is a Hospital Trauma Center located just down the block from the hotel, and for that reason alone, there are certain expectations of noise coming from emergency vehicles at any hour. If someone chooses to stay in a hotel that is right next to a Trauma Center.... *Hello!* He wanted to make sure that the desk clerk noted his complaint.

The next morning I received a call from Mr. A at 7:30 a.m.; it was the last call that I would answer before punching out and heading home. The PBX operator says, "It's Mr. A; he wants to speak to a manager."

I said, "Okay, let me have it."

"Hello, this is the Shift Supervisor Christie. How can I help you Mr. A?"

"You're a manager?"

"Yes I am."

"Can I speak to you in Spanish?"

"No sir, I only speak English."

After a moment of hesitation, perhaps in calculating the thought of what his next move was going to be, he spoke in a very thick Italian accent: "I am a guest of your 'ótel. I come here with an expectation of sleep, and yesterday I have no sleep because a helicopter wake me at 6 a.m. in the morning." His voice got deeper and louder as he psyches himself up during the elocution of his complaint. Mr. A continues, "I have no sleep for two days and I have to go to work! I cannot work without sleep. Today I call my legal advocate and I tell him about this noise. Tomorrow I will leave your 'ótel and I not pay the bill! You understand me?!" Now yelling into my ear at ear-splitting decibels, he repeats himself. "You understand me?! You idiot; you idiot! I no pay! I no pay!" With that he slammed the phone down on the cradle and into my ear.

I put the phone down and with a grimace, I said, "I guess Mr. A just wanted to vent. He says he's not paying because the helicopter woke him up."

Then sarcastically I said, "I guess we just have to call the hospital and ask them to never land another helicopter again."

"I don't care if somebody is on the 'Table' waiting for their lifesaving heart transplant. Let your patient die. Mr. A needs his beauty sleep!"

We all laughed at Mr. A's gall to actually call us on that one. I pulled up Mr. A's file and noted our conversation for the record. Then I wrote a short note to distribute to all of the department heads. Then I went home.

Needless to say, when I arrived to work later on that same night Mr. A had paid his bill in full and there were no adjustments made to his account.

Lady Sings the Blues

We had a famous American female singer who was popular in many genres, including Jazz, Folk, and R & B styles. She was also a Civil Rights Activist. And due to privacy laws and for the purpose of this story, I will refer to her as Ms. S.

After Ms. S finished her evening performance at the world famous Hollywood Bowl Amphitheater, she was tired from expending so much energy, jet lagged, and her body was dealing with being in a different time zone. She was looking forward to a much-needed rest back at her hotel room. She arrived in the lobby looking like the crown jewel in the royal tiara. Her entourage of five or so other people looked like servants to her royal highness. She stopped to momentarily enjoy the humble elegance of the hotel lobby's grand staircase, a focal point of the hotel and object of fascination to many hotel guests. Then she quickly retreated to her hotel room on the tenth floor, home of some of the nicest suites in the building, the Piéce De Résistance of the hotel.

Moments later a call came through to the front desk. Just having arrived to begin my shift at 11 p.m., I answered the call. It was some woman with a thick French accent asking for keys to be brought to Ms. S as she was waiting in the hallway. For some reason, Ms. S's keys weren't opening her door. I, following standard procedure, checked the room number via the computer and found the room was indeed registered to Ms. S so I said, "I'll be glad to send someone with a fresh key. Please show your I.D. to the gentleman I send to your room for guest security reasons before he opens your door."

The voice on the other end of the phone, now quite diplomatically and to the point replied, "Ms. S will not be showing her identification to anyone! Just come and open the door, please."

About that time a young black man dressed in shiny silver clothing and looking quite proper for an awards banquet and sporting an English accent, approached me at the front desk and asked for keys to Ms. S's room. I asked his name and checked to see if it was on the registry of Ms. S's room. It wasn't. I reiterated the hotel's policy on issuing keys to guest's rooms and asked him to comply.

He became distressed and asked the employee that was standing next to me, "You know who I am, don't you? Can you please help me?"

The desk supervisor popped out of the back office to check on the front desk, and I explained to him the situation. He had to decide if a key could be given to this man—this unidentified man who claimed to be with Ms. S. The supervisor grimaced and then reluctantly gave the okay to issue the room key. As the gentleman walked away from the desk, I turned to my supervisor and said, "It's your call, but I wouldn't have given him the key." I asked, "Did you know that guy?"

My supervisor replied, "No I don't, but it's okay."

Not more than five minutes had passed when I answered another phone call from Ms. S's room. The caller, once again the woman with the thick French accent, said, "We asked the housekeeping department to have the room made up when we returned this evening and it hasn't been done. Please don't send anyone now; it's too late and Ms. S is much too tired and can't be disturbed. I will clean the room myself, but can you have a vase and fresh flowers sent up to freshen the room?"

I apologized for the derelict service and said that I would send flowers right away. I hailed the roving houseman on the two-way radio that's kept at the front desk and asked him to deliver the vase and flowers up to Ms. S's room right away.

The houseman answered, "No more vases or flowers tonight. Sorry."

(Rats!) I thought to myself. I took a deep breath of air and then slowly let it out as I debated what could be done to ease the situation. I mean, first of all I gave the entourage a hard time about issuing the keys to the room and kept Ms. S waiting around in the hallway. Then her room hasn't been cleaned after she left specific instructions for it to be done, and now the houseman is telling me that the hotel is fresh out of vases and flowers!

Now I'm realizing the importance of just who Ms. S is and her impact on this particular French hotel. So I'm thinking, *where do I find fresh flowers at 2 a.m. in the morning?* Just then I see the answer! The front desk has two beautiful and very expensive orchid arrangements in terra cotta glazed pots sitting on the counter, one on each end of the desk. I called the bellman over to the desk, and upon his arrival I promptly put a pot in his hands and said, "Deliver this to Ms. S's room right away." The bellman looked at me as if I was insane, and then he shrugged his shoulders and went on about his task. I chuckled under my breath as the bellman walked away with that flower pot in his hands. I thought to myself, *I must be some kind of a nut to pull that off! So how am I going to explain the missing pot to the morning manager?* Oh well, it's all in a day's work!

If necessity is the mother of invention, then resourcefulness is the father.

~ Beulah Louise Henry

The Squared Circle

I've been a pro wrestling fan since before I could walk. My grandfather took my mother to live matches when she was just a kid, and my mother in turn took me to live matches when I was growing up, and I in turn took my kids to live matches. So I've always been a wrestling fan.

One morning as I was just about to clock out and go home, we were informed that a rather large group was checking out, and so they asked me if I could stay just a few minutes later to help out. Within minutes most of the group had checked out and were waiting for transportation to the airport. As I looked around the lobby, I couldn't help but notice that several of these guests looked all too familiar. I finished up helping and decided to take a closer look.

To my astonishment and utter excitement, the lobby was full of my professional wrestling heroes! Wrestling legends! They were all there!

- The Russian Bear, Ivan Koloff;
- Mr. Wonderful, Paul Orndorff;
- Greg "The Hammer" Valentine;
- Koko B. Ware;
- B. Brian Blair of "The Killer Bees;"
- The Honky Tonk Man, Irwin R. Schyster (IRS);
- Colonel DeBeers; and
- The Iron Sheik!

I was star stuck. To me these guys were more like my family because I had grown up following all of their careers, both on television and in live matches.

The hotel frowns on any type of interaction that isn't business related, like say, asking for an autograph; but here were my heroes and I wasn't going to pass up this opportunity to say "Hello." They were all so friendly and outgoing, and I got goosebumps as I was talking with them about their greatest matches of which many I had personally witnessed. Greg Valentine asked me why I hadn't asked for his autograph, and I explained that it was against hotel policy for me to do so. Greg basically said, "To Hell with policy! Get me a piece of paper!" All the girls were swooning over Mr. Wonderful, and he just kept mentioning how much he loved and was devoted to Mrs. Wonderful.

IRS was the only one that seemed to be rude and had an attitude problem, but who cared about that? The rest of the gang was absolutely awesome!

Their shuttle bus finally arrived, and as they were filing out of the lobby, they shook hands, signed autographs, and snapped pictures with their fans. What a memorable day for all of us!

There's no drama like wrestling.

~ Kane

Chapter 3: Drunks and Whack Jobs

Rowdy Women

Often times we get drunk obnoxious people who are not guests of the hotel and just wander through the lobby and use the restroom. And sometimes they are just up to no good.

One night in particular a man and a woman found their way into the hotel lobby around 3 a.m. in the morning. The woman was clutching a bottle of alcohol and was being very loud and obnoxious. The Security Officer Gustavo was called in to keep an eye on the pair. They walked up to the second floor bathrooms and went in. Gustavo couldn't tell if they had both gone into the ladies room, but he just had a gut feeling about it. He waited for about five minutes chatting with the night houseman, who was sweeping the floors but also doubled as a security guard on Gustavo's nights off. The man reappeared after five minutes, but again Gustavo couldn't be sure of what restroom he had used. He didn't see the woman he was with, either. Gustavo followed the man back to the lobby, and then shortly thereafter the woman also reappeared. They both went into the lobby and sat down and put their feet up on the glass table and continued their rather boisterous conversation.

Gustavo approached the pair and asked them to please quiet down as it was 3 a.m. in the morning and other guests were sleeping. The woman said, "Are you Cuban?" and "Who are you to be telling me to quiet down? I'll be as loud as I want; do you understand?"

About that time a call came over the radio for someone to attend to the ladies room on the second floor. When Gustavo got there the entire restroom had been trashed! Paper towels and toilet paper were everywhere and water from the sink was overflowing onto the restroom floor. So that's why the woman had taken so long in the restroom. She was being drunk and mischievous. As Gustavo returned from the restroom, the man and woman were still being loud and obnoxious so I was called in to handle the situation.

I approached the pair with Gustavo backing me up. I confronted her about the fact that she had trashed the ladies room and I said that she was asked very nicely to keep her voice down and keep her feet off of the tables. Now it was time for them to leave since they had caused general mayhem and were NOT guests of the hotel. I explained that the local police department had been contacted and were in route to arrest them for being drunk in public and for vandalism to the hotel. The woman stood up and quieted down and asked for a taxi. I directed them to the valet parking attendant, who would hail a cab for them. The taxi arrived shortly and the two of them got in and drove off into the night.

When dealing with a drunken person, we had to have a firm hand and use extreme diplomacy so that the situation wouldn't get out of control. Most drunks do have enough self-control to know right from wrong, and they don't want to wind up with matching bracelets courtesy of Los Angeles' finest. Getting drunk and causing trouble is just a big *No-No* in my book!

Manic Depression Is Still in my Head

On January 2, Ms. Andrews checked into hotel room 1007. The desk agent that checked her in had noted that Ms. Andrews had exhibited what she believed to be rather eccentric behavior. Apparently the guest was dancing and singing loudly in the lobby area.

It was noted during the night audit that Ms. Andrews had made a purchase in the gift shop of less than $2.00 and yet left a $100.00 tip. She also ordered room service and had an order of less than $10.00, and it was noted that she had also left room service a $100.00 tip on the receipt. When the room service attendant was approached concerning the tip, it was mentioned that the guest authorized that they put an appropriate tip on the ticket.

Ms. Andrews called the hotel operator around 3 a.m. and ordered tea. She was asked whether or not she had knowledge of the rather generous tips. She replied no and stated that she would normally give a $3.00 tip. Later the room service attendant attempted to deliver tea to her room. He received no answer from the guest room. Around 3:15 a.m. Ms. Andrews called down from her room again to order tea. This time she spoke in French.

About fifteen minutes after the second phone call for tea, Ms. Andrews appeared in the lobby. She appeared to be extremely disoriented and in a state of agitation. She began babbling incoherently to herself while talking on a cell phone. At one point she handed her cell phone to a guest and then to the night auditor, André. It was at this point that André made contact with Ms. Andrews' sister Dee Dee. She explained to André that her sister was a manic depressive and had been off of her meds. She also expressed concern for her sister's well-being and asked if we would call the police so that she would be isolated and receive the medication that she needed. Ms. Andrews then took the phone back and proceeded to wander about the lobby aimlessly. She then walked outside, returned, and went back to her room.

No more than five minutes later, Ms. Andrews once again called down to the hotel operator and began singing and babbling over the house phone. Both night auditors on duty discussed calling the police and decided that it would be in the best interest of everyone concerned if the police were called in to handle the situation. Ms. Andrews reappeared in the lobby moments later and the tenth floor fire alarms were going off! Ms. Andrews had pulled the alarm before coming back down to the lobby. The switchboard lit up with guest calls and concerns. We reassured them that it was a false alarm and alerted security.

Fifteen minutes later the LAPD arrived and agreed to speak with Ms. Andrews. When they attempted to make contact, Ms. Andrews barricaded herself in her room. The police finally gained entrance to the room and were assaulted upon making contact with Ms. Andrews. She was then taken into custody. I notified Ms. Andrews' family and relayed information to them as to her location and the process that the police would follow. I said that any other questions or concerns could be addressed by our hotels security department.

Ms. Andrews was taken to a local Los Angeles hospital and put under a 72-hour psychiatric hold and was given proper medication. And as far as I knew she was back home safe and sound and doing well.

We just never knew what we were going to run up against on the graveyard shift when there was generally only a skeleton crew on staff.

Gypsies, Tramps, and Thieves

When the weather starts getting colder, the transients that are homeless, mentally ill, and sometimes drunk or drug addicted come wandering into the hotel in the middle of the night. And believe me when I say we get our fair share of all of the above individuals. Here is one man's story:

A transient man wandered into the hotel around 12:30 a.m. He wasn't wearing any shoes, his pants were falling off, he was disheveled, and he smelled bad. He seemed to be quite incoherent, and he drove up to the valet area in a run-down vehicle that was loaded with trash from fast-food restaurants and other personal belongings. He walked up to the front desk and presented me with an unsigned credit card and asked for the "best room in the house." When asked to present his ID, he claimed that his wallet had been stolen earlier that evening; however they didn't get his credit card (how convenient). Without ID, we were unable to honor his credit card, for guests' privacy and safely reasons. He continually asked for a glass of water, and I declined to give him one due to his obvious mental instability. I was feeling very nervous and I feared for my safety, so I asked our hotel security to come up and remove him from the premises.

The gentleman wandered through the lobby and began rattling the house phone in the lobby. Doug, our security officer, continually asked the man to leave with no compliance from the man. So Doug asked me to call the police and report a mentally unstable transient in the hotel. The police said that they would arrive just as soon as someone was available. It seemed that all the available units were busy dealing with two separate shootings in Los Angeles, and it would be some time before they could free up a unit.

Now the bellman, Francis, and the valet, Miguel, were all involved; and between the three of them (Doug, Francis, and Miguel) after much coaxing the gentleman finally left the property. The transient himself called the police and informed them that it was we who were harassing him! Everyone went back to their stations, and as Doug was watching the security cameras he noticed the gentleman was headed back into the hotel. Doug asked me to give the police another call.

The police finally arrived, and by that time the gentleman had left the property and walked across the street to a gas station. We gave the officers a description of the man so they went to the gas station and questioned the man and at that time decided to take him into custody. For what reason I never found out, but I was just glad to have him out of my lobby and I was feeling safe again.

This brings to mind a general consensus concerning the intoxicated, mentally ill, and drug-influenced individuals. It does not matter if they are rich or poor, clean or disheveled. If our safety is in question, security needs to be prepared to act with caution and understanding of the situation and stay in the area until the situation is completely under control.

Play Me a Song; I'm the Piano Man

Quite a few hotels have pianos in their lobbies. Sometimes the pianos are automatic-player pianos, and sometimes a professional pianist will be hired to play for a few peak hours during the day and early evening, and some just have the piano for looks. Our hotel had a grand piano in the lobby, and during the day the piano's keyboard was unlocked and anyone who could play a tune was welcome to try. Once in a blue moon, there would be a truly great piano player; and sometimes someone with a beautiful voice would jump in and start singing along. But most guests were amateur players and we usually ended up hearing the "Knuckle Song" or "Heart and Soul," another popular beginner tune played.

One particular busy night we had several banquets going on, and there were many requests made to the front desk and all other departments. We were literally flying by the seat of our pants! One of the events was titled "Beautiful," although I don't remember exactly what they were celebrating that night. My coworkers and I only knew that a rather large group of people had broken off from the banquet, hit the bar, and were now situated around the piano... and then someone started to play.

The guests were playing loudly and painfully singing along. In our nightly report to management, we stated that we could only take bad Stevie Wonder for two hours, not four. We had asked security to ask the *fun-loving* party goers to tone it down just a bit but to no avail. The singers didn't end up leaving until 4 a.m. The bar closed at 2 a.m., and that is the time when someone should have access to the piano key lock. Apparently the security officer did not have such a key.

It is fun to play a piano and make memories, but a piano in a hotel lobby is not for karaoke and mediocre singers. They should definitely not be singing for several hours in a hotel lobby… and to wee hours in the morning! Save it for the shower.

The Valentina Law Suit

Early one Tuesday morning around 3 a.m., a woman approached the front desk and asked me if I would check to see if we were holding a complimentary room in her name. She identified herself as Ms. Senecal, and we were in fact NOT holding a complimentary room for her. She then said that the room may have been under a different name, and she proceeded to give several names, none of which were showing in our reservations. Ms. Senecal then admitted that she was currently involved in litigation with several of the movie and television studios in Los Angeles and that her attorney, whom she failed to identify, was arranging a complimentary room for her because she was currently living in her car. Again I told Ms. Senecal that we were NOT holding a reservation for her and she then left the premises.

Wednesday morning Ms. Senecal returned once again and presented André with a handwritten law suit naming all litigants involved in her suit with our in-house restaurant being one of the litigants named in her suit (page 3). She asked that this document be forwarded to the general manager because "He should know about these people!" Here is just a partial list of complaints from her 8-page manifesto that she titled the "Valentina Law suit:"

- Life destruction by these people: murder, arson, and grand theft

49

- Victimized, tortured, and attempted murder (Address given)
- Poisoned fruit
- Mail transfers, stolen mail
- Messages erased, phone machine broken
- Poisoned, murdered sheepdog
- Murdered brother
- Breaking and entering
- Personal items stolen
- Wrongful termination
- Wrongful eviction
- Sexual harassment by my neighbor

She went on to name the following persons as the people that she is suing:

- Texas A & M
- Pretty woman
- Thelma and Louise
- NASCAR movie, Stallone
- Dr. Zhivago
- Beauty and the Beast
- The Little Mermaid
- Pippi Long-stocking
- Mork and Mindy
- Black Beauty
- The Ghostbusters
- Harold and Maude

And the list went on. I will spare you the painful details as Ms. Senecal appears to have been a mentally unstable person who should be under some sort of medical care.

Upon analyzing the handwritten document, I am sure that we can dismiss this woman's complaint as unrealistic, at best. However, since she seemed to have our establishment on her list of agendas, we needed to be prepared for any repercussions.

We never did hear from Ms. Senecal again after that day. I only hope that she was able to get the attention and help that she needed.

Hell in a Hand Basket

Occasionally we had a group of partiers who after attending a function in one of our banquet rooms would want to continue the party after the banquet hall closed down at 2 a.m. Usually they would wind up in one of their hotel rooms. Someone makes a liquor run about 1:30 a.m. so that the after-party is well stocked. And since everyone is feeling no pain, someone inevitably asks, "Where is the music?" Bam! Now there is a party going on.

But the guests in the neighboring hotel rooms haven't been invited to the party and are not exactly appreciative. The music, the loud voices, and sometimes the loud crashing sounds coming from the party room are very annoying at 3 a.m. in the morning when people are trying to sleep. So we as hotel staff, after getting the complaint calls, call our hotel security to tell the partiers to quiet down. Sometimes it takes several visits from our security office to quiet people down. Once in a while we get a real rowdy bunch that refuse to quiet down, and at that point we have to call in the police department.

Other times the ruckus is a domestic spat between a husband and a wife or girlfriend and boyfriend. Lovers' quarrels can be super emotionally charged and can get dangerous when escalated, as was the case of Dr. Wiley in room 428. Someone in room 430, which was right next door, called to report a loud argument in the adjacent room. The guest said that it sounded serious. I sent our security officer, Doug, to check it out, and Doug said that when Dr. Wiley answered the door that he had a black eye and visible scratches on his face, and the good doctor slammed the door in Doug's face! Ten minutes later, a young girl no more than twelve or thirteen approached the front desk crying and said, "Can I get some help in room 428? My mom and I want to leave the hotel and my dad won't let us. He keeps pushing my mom around."

Doug was already outside of the room and called me via the house phone by the elevators and asked me to call the police, indicating that the situation seemed to be escalating. I dialed 911 and said that we appear to have a domestic altercation in progress. The Los Angeles Police Department arrived within ten minutes of the call.

Twenty minutes later the LAPD walked through the lobby with the woman, presumably Dr. Wiley's wife, in handcuffs. The situation was handled but not without interrupting and annoying other hotel guests.

When people get to a hotel, they just want to relax, unwind, and have a decent night's sleep without being woken up at some ungodly hour because of noise, whatever that noise may be. We as hotel staff do our best to handle the situations ourselves, but sometimes we have to call in the experts. In those cases, when guests have lodged a complaint during the night, it is appropriate to ask about getting some sort of discount or other compensation for the disruption. Usually, hotel staff has no problem relocating, upgrading, or discounting our guests' room for that reason.

Another Busy Day of Being Insane

Wow, it's just so hard to believe that certain individuals can be so profoundly mentally ill to where they really can't take care of themselves or they become a danger to others. This is one of those stories.

The guest in room 825 had been displaying some rather erratic behavior since arriving to our hotel. She was a "walk-in" guest and had been paying for her charges with large cash deposits on a daily basis.

52

One night she continued calling the front desk and PBX ranting and raving about how she is the messiah and she had sex with an angel and her child is the anti-Christ. She also claimed to be Hitler reincarnated and had all the keys to the world's knowledge. Later on in the evening she came into the lobby with green foam on her mouth. Out of concern we called the paramedics. She refused treatment and the paramedics left. Twenty minutes later she came bolting through the lobby and tried to enter a guest vehicle in the valet parking area as the guest was arriving. She physically accosted our guest Mr. Pappas in room 936 and left scratches on his arms. She entered the guest elevators and spilled pills all over the elevator and then attacked another guest, Ms. Mohamed, who was also on the elevator with her small child. She grabbed the child and terribly frightened Ms. Mohamed. She also threatened the lives of the staff verbally and grabbed the clothing of Francis, the bellman, and tried to tear his radio from him.

We called 911 a second and third time. As we made the calls, she ran outside into oncoming traffic and was nearly hit by several vehicles. She then ran to the Mobile gas station and tried to enter several vehicles there as well, and the Mobile gas station attendant also called 911. By the time the LAPD had arrived, she was nowhere to be found.

She had not returned to our hotel and we had taken measures to keep her out of her room until the LAPD could arrive and take her into custody. We LOCKED her out and updated everyone concerning the situation.

Communication with all the staff was imperative. This is what we made sure everyone knew:

She should NOT be allowed back into her room. When calling the LAPD, inform them that we are detaining a 415 (Disturbing the peace) and we need a return call from officers. We also feel strongly that this guest should be asked to leave the hotel immediately and NOT return because she is a danger to everyone. I don't think the hotel wants to incur any liability.

Secret Agent Man

A homeless man wandered into the lobby and went into the men's restroom. He was there for quite a while. Our security guard, Francis, went to investigate and found that not only did the homeless man trash the men's restroom but he was also curled up into a fetal position and was asleep in one of the stalls. Francis woke him up and escorted him out of the building.

Also a drunk walked in asking how to get to Wilshire Boulevard, flashed a business card that said that he was some sort of US Special Forces investigator, and then he demanded to see my identification immediately. I called for security because this guy literally reeked of alcohol. The security officer, Alan, who is Filipino, showed up and then the man produced a key chain that had a Philippine logo on it and he began speaking in Tagalog to Alan, again asking for my identification. I informed the drunken man that I don't give my identification to anyone. Being that he was obviously inebriated, I asked him if he had a room here and if not, was he planning on taking a room here at our weekend rate. He said no and at that point I had Alan escort the gentleman off of the property. He left without any further incident.

We got all kinds when I worked in a busy hotel in a busy part of town. It was important to just know how to "roll with the punches."

The Scam of the Century

One afternoon a customer called the hotel and asked for the GM or general manager. Now the GM is the highest rank possible in the hotel, and the GM's usually live in suites on the highest floor of the hotel. Our GM was a man named Dana Robert Fenek, so if one didn't know that he was a man, one might innocently assume that he was a woman, especially since Dana is more traditionally a woman's name. Anyhow, a customer had called the hotel at about 4 o'clock that afternoon, and I happened to catch the call at the front desk. The customer had a male voice and he asked if he could speak to the GM, Dana. I told him that Dana was currently on vacation in Hawaii and wouldn't be back for another ten days. He then asked if "She" had left any special instructions in "Her" absence. I immediately corrected the man and said that Dana wasn't a "She". He seemed a little caught off guard by that. I informed him that as far as I knew, no special instructions had been left by our GM. I asked if there was anything else that I could help him with and he said "No" and then he ended the call. No big deal but a little odd that he didn't know that Dana was a man.

Later on that night at about 10 o'clock I again caught a call about the GM at the front desk. As I answered the call, I happened to notice that the voice that I was hearing was the same male voice that had inquired about the GM Dana earlier in the day and had inquired about special instructions. I didn't let the caller know this because something was telling me that this was going to be an interesting call, and I was wondering how it would play out. The caller went on to identify himself by name although I don't recall his name because it's been quite a few years since then. The caller stated that he was just blocks away from the hotel and he had a caravan of cars with him. He stated that GM Dana had arranged for him and his party to stay for a week in the Presidential suite at no charge to him. I informed him that I was aware of no such provision for anyone by his name and that there was no way that I could verify that information at this particular time of the evening.

He said, "Look I just got off the phone with your GM Dana Fenek." "I know that he is in Hawaii and he told me that all the arrangements had been made and that all I had to do was to mention his name and that everything would be taken care of. If you don't believe me, then why don't you call him yourself?"

I said, "It's much too late to call Mr. Fenek now, but I'll be happy to call him and verify your story in the morning." At that point the caller began to get a little heated and started to threaten me with getting fired as well as taking legal action against me personally. Well, this had me somewhat alarmed because what if what he was telling me was actually true? However, something in my gut told me that this guy was just trying to run some sort of a scam to get into a Presidential suite for free and probably throw an "off the hook" party up there with God knows what kind of damage to the room when it got out of control. It sounded strange because it was the same voice that didn't know that Dana was a man earlier; and if he was such good friends with Dana, he certainly should have known that he was in fact a man.

I put the caller on a brief hold and had informed my supervisor of what the caller was asking for, told him about the call earlier, and told him that I thought this guy was trying to pull a fast one on us! My supervisor agreed with me but he said, "Tell them to go ahead and come down here and I'll call the local authorities and have them waiting for him when he gets here. So I got back on the phone and I did just as my supervisor had advised me and we put our plan into motion.

True to his word, a literal caravan of vehicles pulled up into the valet parking area, and then people began spilling out and walking into the lobby. The man with the familiar voice approached me at the front desk, and I went through the motions of having him fill out a registration card but he refused to show me his ID or leave a form of payment. As this was happening I happened to notice several uniformed Los Angeles police officers walking into the lobby, and they were met by my supervisor, who filled them in on all the details. The officers then approached the man with the familiar voice and promptly slapped the cuffs on him. Everyone that was in his party was also arrested.

The officers had later informed us that this particular crew of hoodlums had been scamming several other hotels in the vicinity with the same scam. They also said that several of the vehicles that they were driving had been reported as "stolen."

The officers thanked us for our quick thinking and for being smart enough to not fall for their crazy story.

Mr. Jones, I Presume?

The guest, Mr. Marks in room 621, was a walk-in on a cash-only basis with a government rate of $115.00. The new desk agent took a deposit for one night; and the following day the guest extended for one additional night, and no additional deposit was collected by the desk agents.

This guest seemed very familiar to some of the veteran desk agents, and after some discussion we determined that this guest may be affiliated with another Mr. Marks that regularly attempts to walk in with ID that does not match the credit card and also makes reservations under different names each time he attempts to stay. Once checked in, these particular guests are extremely hard on our rooms making it a very difficult job for the housekeepers to clean the mess that they create. Furthermore, they always seem to go directly to the new front desk agents who are not as detail-oriented as our veteran desk agents and who are not as likely to catch on to someone trying to misrepresent themselves in an attempt to defraud our establishment.

The new desk agents needed to be thoroughly versed on our policy regarding walk-in guests, including available rates for the current day and that certain rates must be arranged prior to check-in through our in-house reservations department and NOT negotiated at the time of check-in by the guest trying to get a better rate.

A Cold Night in December

When guests have a bad experience in a reputable hotel, they naturally get angry and feel as if they are owed some sort of compensation. When the compensation isn't good enough for them, they inevitably play the "I can make one phone call and ruin your life" card. Generally those empty threats are just that—

empty threats. Nevertheless, a member of management should be called in to deal with the situation.

Guest Daniel E in room 933 was moved from room 312 due to the loud fan noise that has been a consistent problem on the third floor for weeks now. This guest stayed with us every month for five days at a time, and he said the last time he was here he had a bad experience with a very rude female front desk agent. He said that he knows people at the corporate offices in France, and one simple phone call would fix everything for us! He said he will never stay here again because of his two bad experiences in a row. He wanted his room refunded for the night of December 2 of which I had already done. He wanted his report of what happened, i.e., the noise, written down officially because he didn't not want to repeat himself to other managers or desk agents. He further suggested that I upgrade him to a junior suite because his sleep was so valuable that we could not possibly put a price on it to repay him. I advised him that we would do everything within reason to accommodate him, and that I would pass his information on to management for further consideration.

If this guest actually knew anyone at corporate headquarters in France, of that I couldn't be sure. So I left it to management to sort it all out. Of course we all had a good laugh at his folly.

Strangers in the Night

A man claiming to be a Pacific Bell Telephone repairman arrived at the hotel at about 12 a.m. He said that Pac Bell alerted him that our telephone system was down; and we were apparently running on our back-up system, and he was here to run a test and make the necessary repairs. We asked to see his ID, and he presented a Pac Bell ID badge with a photo identifying him as M. Santos.

We asked if he was here for the ZETA phone system support due to the phantom phone calls in guests' rooms. He did not know who ZETA was nor did he know about the phantom phone calls. We called Security Officer Doug and Doug once again asked to see the man's ID. He asked the man a few more questions to determine his exact purpose here at the hotel. The man said he needed access to the main telephone room. We were unsure of where that was so we showed him the switchboard in the computer room. He said that was not the correct location. Doug then showed the man the main telephone room located elsewhere in the hotel. It was during that time that we thought it would be a good idea to contact David, the engineering manager, as a precautionary measure.

David answered our page almost immediately; and when briefed on the situation, he indicated that he had no prior knowledge either from Pac Bell or anyone else that there was a problem with the phones or that a repairman would be on the premises at such an odd hour. David had great concerns with this Pac Bell repairman being on the property and thought it could be a person or organization with ulterior motives to cause harm to our hotel.

David asked us to escort the man off of the property and tell him to come back during regular daytime business hours. Doug went to escort the man off of the property, but the man said that he had already fixed the problem. He said that a communication card had gone bad, and he merely replaced it with a new one.

It was highly unusual to have a repair person on property without prior notification from any manager. However, there have been repair personnel on the property during the hours of midnight until 5 a.m. in past history. We all felt a little uneasy about this particular repairman. We attempted to contact Pac Bell to verify the man's employment, but all the numbers were either not available or had messages giving their regular business hours.

It would be advisable for someone to follow up on the employment verification of said repairman and also do a thorough check of the area in which the man was working. We've all seen movies and TV shows where highly technical people try to hack into computer systems and have made fake ID's to obtain access to computer databases and phone lines for the purposes of wiretapping and illegal recording. I don't know if that's what happened that night. But it still left an uneasy feeling in the pits of our stomachs.

Technological progress is like an axe in the hands of a pathological criminal.

~ Albert Einstein

Chapter 4: Odds and Ends

The One Button

The main goal of the night auditor is to check that all the numbers are correct and in the right columns before running the end-of-day program at around 2:30 a.m. At that time they shut down the main computer and run what we affectionately call "The One Button" which zeros out the end of day and resets everything for the following day. The program then prints out an encyclopedia set of reports that get distributed to every department in the hotel.

On this particular night there were problems. One of the front desk agents, who was rather new to be hotel staff, had accidentally started the "One Button" at around 3 p.m. that afternoon! When the agents couldn't get into the computer for regular check-ins and such, the manager realized that the "One Button" had started and he quickly shut it down by re-booting the mainframe. But the damage had already been done. When I arrived at 11 p.m. that night, the manager had informed me as to what had happened and wished me luck on the night audit. Now I basically had two sets of numbers that I had to reconcile, and when I ran the audit I had to explain the extreme differences in the numbers and try to make it make sense.

I was on the phone most of the night with technical support in New York trying to explain to them what had happened, and they tried to fix it for me. After hours in a conference call with software experts, they finally came up with a viable solution. But it had run way past our 2:30 a.m. deadline. So I had to run the actual "One Button" at 6:30 a.m. the next morning which kept the mainframe off-line well into the morning check-out rush. That meant that guests left the hotel without their final bills and without their final credit card payments processed. This naturally made for some bad mojo from the guests in the morning—especially those that had to have final paperwork to submit to their corporate business accounts.

Later on in the morning when the mainframe came back on line, we had a mountain of paperwork to do and credit cards to authorize and then either mail out the completed bills to the guests or fax copies to their offices. Needless to say I got a hell of a lot of overtime pay that day, and by the time I made it home that afternoon I was spent.

Random information

Some big hotels have safety deposit boxes for the convenience of their guests, and some big hotels also have safety deposit boxes for their front desk staff. Management generally wants the front desk to start off with a $1000 bank because people need change and cash personal checks and do another myriad of financial transactions throughout the day. The front desk manager often has a bank worth anywhere from $10,000 to $25,000, and there is usually an airline manager specifically designated for the many flight crews, pilots, and flight attendants who check in and are given a daily per diem of several hundred dollars for meals and what not. That bank is easily $10,000 to $15,000 as well. So if you've got five to seven front desk agents and two managers all on duty at the same time, one can see how much money is floating around at any one time. It could be upwards of $40,000— definitely an enticement to any would-be robbers with a well thought-out plan. That's one of the reasons I was always a little on edge while I was working there. And security, surveillance cameras, and unarmed guard patrols—well, that was generally a joke. Believe me I've thought this through on many a night.

You've also got the odd-ball employees who think it's cool to go on their lunch breaks and sneak up to a dirty room from a late checkout that housekeeping won't be servicing until the next morning, to take snacks out of the minibars, and catch the first half of a pay-per-view movie only to have it charged to the former guest. Employees have even been known to have "quickie" sexual liaisons with other hotel employees in dirty unoccupied rooms while on their breaks. Shocking, I know, but this stuff really happens a lot more than one would think.

One nice perk of working in a hotel with world-class chefs on staff is that we get to talk to them, usually at the beginning or ending of our shift and sometimes get to taste their latest and greatest creations. Often, we even get first-hand impromptu cooking lessons.

Sometimes the hotel makes the local gym facilities available for free to hotel employees to use on their off time.

There is the added bonus as I stated earlier about the opportunity to stay in the hotel at extremely discounted rates, like almost next to nothing, and I certainly made the most out of that perk. I was always putting up my visiting relatives in fancy four-star hotels.

The Name Game

One thing about working in a hotel and meeting people from all over the world is that we come access some pretty odd last names. Here's just a few of the really notable ones:

- Mr. Death
- Mr. Gordo (a rather obese gentleman)
- Mr. Small (a gentleman who was under 4 feet tall)

63

- Mr. Casebeer
- Ms. Cherry Berry
- Mr. Li suk yoo (he was from Indonesia)
- Mr. Long and Mr. Tongue (traveling together). I checked their ID's.
- Mr. Pedo (which is the Spanish word for FART)

I couldn't avoid the compelling desire to ask to see the guests ID when I came across an unusual name. My supervisor Juan was checking Mr. Pedo in and had to excuse himself from finishing the check-in because Juan was Colombian and Spanish was his first language, and he just couldn't maintain his composure when he realized that he was checking in Mr. Fart. Juan had a riotous laugh in the back office for about ten minutes. Yeah, I guess you could say that my supervisor dropped the ball on that one.

Another thing that happens most notably is that we have to deal with rude customers, and here are some of the sneaky things a front desk agent can do to a guest that is exceptionally rude or snooty to them, especially when you're acting polite and very professional towards them:

- Give the guest a room down at the very end of a long hallway.
- Put them into a room next to the elevators or ice machines so that they won't get a peaceful night's rest.
- I've even put them into rooms directly underneath the helicopter landing pad.

So it pays to be nice to your desk agent. Just saying.

A lot of times guests have special requests, like to be on a ground floor, or to have something special waiting for them in their room, like a bouquet of flowers, a fruit basket, a bottle of Don Pérignon, and a plate of chocolate-covered strawberries. Some hotels that allow pets to stay will get a special pet package that includes pet treats and toys. Other guests have food allergies and can only drink special milk or other special foods that aren't on the menu and aren't usually stocked by the kitchen crew. So when we see one of those regulars, we take petty cash out of the till and send a bellman off to the local organic grocery store to purchase it. Hotel staff will bust their butts to accommodate their guests to make sure that they have an absolutely unforgettable experience in their hotel.

Random Gifts

One thing that the hotels frown upon is guests giving employees tokens of their affections. We are specifically told not to accept any kind or manner of gratuity from a guest with the exceptions of bellmen, waiters, bartenders, and waitresses. Then it's okay, but they should only be receiving tips and not material gifts.

I've often gotten around that rule by quickly hiding it in an empty drawer or putting it, if it's small enough, into one of my pockets. Some of the cool stuff that past guests have given me are: bottles of alcohol, wine, champagne, and even whiskey. I've received tickets to concerts and Broadway plays. On two separate occasions, real-life astronauts have given me official NASA mission patches that have been worn on their space suits. A world champion bull rider gave me an autographed trading card that had his picture on the front and a brief bio on the back of the card along with his statistics. I've received $1.00 coins from almost every country in the world. It's a great collection that I truly cherish. Once I was given a set of four coffee mugs with American Flags on them. I was given several programs from concerts and events; one of them was the program from the first-ever annual Latin Grammy Awards show. I've received Christmas cards and thank you cards from all over the world. A few guests wanted me to pose in pictures with them and later on they sent copies of the picture back to me. I don't like to offend a guest or make them feel awkward or embarrassed by turning down a gift. After all, it makes them feel good to do a little something for me, especially since I was one of the employees that made their stay extra special.

At one point we had a guest that had been living at our hotel for over three years. He was in poor health and couldn't get around that well. The bell staff would go up to his room on a nightly basis and help him bathe himself, put on clean clothes, and put him to bed. The room service crew would bring his food and sit with him and spoon feed him so he wouldn't starve to death. The housekeepers did their part too. He was a very nice gentleman, and we didn't mind going the extra mile for him, and we expected nothing in return. His name was Morgan, and he was reportedly related to the famous business tycoon J.P. Morgan.

Well, after three years in the hotel. Mr. Morgan passed quietly in his sleep. We were all shocked; and some, who had worked closely with him, were devastated by his passing.

A few weeks later several of my coworkers received official looking letters from a high-powered attorney's office. The letters stated that Mr. Morgan had left a "Last will and testament," and that they were being asked to attend the reading of the will. In that meeting it was confirmed that Mr. Morgan had been so grateful for the service and care that he received and for the friendships that he had forged, that he was leaving a sum of one million dollars to each of the employees that had helped and befriended him. We found it both exciting and unbelievable, because as I stated before, we were caring for him out of the kindness of our hearts, and we were not expecting anything in return.

Of course Mr. Morgan's family had much to say about that and the will and his estate were tied up in the courts for years. Ultimately, none of the individually named employees ever received a dime from Mr. Morgan's estate. But it was just a good feeling to know how much we had meant to our friend and our special guest.

Phone Ghosts and Floods

I've never known a hotel that had so many plumbing problems and mysterious phone glitches.

It seems that the telephones like to ring in the guest rooms in the middle of the night waking their occupants from their deepest slumber only to hear nothing but a dial tone on the other end. Then, obviously perturbed, the guest will hang up and settle back into their slumber only to be awoken again moments later with the same resulting dial tone. Now justifiably angered, and a tad bit mystified, they call down to the front desk to inquire whether or not someone has been trying to contact them. When it has been confirmed that no one has been trying to contact them, they inform the desk agent of the events that have just occurred with their telephone and promptly lodge a complaint. Those at the front desk have to take care to note that it is an ungodly hour of the morning, that the guests were soundly sleeping, and that they have only mere hours before their scheduled wake-up call for their early flight or meeting or what not.

The desk agent then explains to the disturbed guest that the phone system has a glitch. And that the technicians have been made aware of the problem and are currently working to correct it. In the meantime the guest telephones have two buttons on them identified as "Line 1" and "Line 2." They are assured that by simply depressing completely down one of those buttons, their silence should temporarily be restored. At which point the desk agent usually hears an abrupt "click," the sound of disconnection. A lot of times the guest will call right back and apologize for disconnecting, saying that they pressed one of the "line" buttons.

The second problem is the plumbing. There are so many complaints of toilets not working or running or backing up. Once I had a guest who was running water in the bathtub, and she stepped away to make a quick phone call. When she returned to the bathroom, she found the tub empty and water an inch deep on the bathroom floor! On the graveyard shift generally considered 11 p.m. to 7 a.m., there are usually no supervisors on duty and all the departments are closed with the exception of the front desk, security, the hotel bar, and one roving housekeeper to take care of simple guest requests like extra pillows and towels. So when plumbing problems occur during the night, the only recourse is to move the guest to another room and mark the problem room as "Out-of-order" until hotel maintenance can fix it in the morning.

Every once in a while, we get an irate guest who doesn't want to move and demands that someone fix the problem immediately. When that happens, it's a lottery drawing for who gets to go and deal with the dilemma. Once the night auditor, a hotel accountant who only works graveyard at the front desk, got the luck of the draw! On his way to the elevator he passed two front desk agents who were on their way to punch out and go home. One of the agents, a blondish-brown-haired pretty girl, said to the night auditor, "I hope you don't find a floater!" The auditor said, "I hope I don't either." The two front desk agents laughed and went into a frenzy of "shit" jokes. The auditor balked at them and headed up to the guests room. Luckily all that was required was a quick plunge and the auditor never mentioned if he did or did not find a "floater".

Smoking Guest

In this day and age, everyone wants respect, including the smokers versus the non-smokers. It's gotten so bad that we've actually passed laws and created city ordinances that forbid smoking in most places and created designated smoking areas for those of us that choose to "light up," to the detriment of our health. Hotels now have non-smoking rooms and in some cases entire smoke-free floors which give about a 25% to 75% mix with the smokers getting the lesser of the percentage. Surprisingly, a lot of smokers request non-smoking rooms because they don't like the smell of the stale cigarettes in their rooms. Usually the hotel will run out of non-smoking rooms and have only smoking rooms left for those late arrivals, and of course, the guests always have something to say about it.

"I specifically requested a non-smoking room when I made my reservation. If I knew that I couldn't have a non-smoking room, I would have made arrangements to stay elsewhere!"

To which the guest will get the standard smoking spiel in return:

- "Non-smoking rooms are offered as a courtesy to our guests."
- "They are not guaranteed."
- "They are given on a first-come first-serve basis."
- "If after you've inspected your room and you find it too smoky or smelly, we can send up some air freshener to help you make it through the night and tomorrow afternoon you can stop by the front desk about 2 p.m. and we can move you to a non-smoking room for the remainder of your stay."

Occasionally, and actually it is more of a rare occurrence, the hotel will sell out of smoking rooms, thus the smoker is forced to abstain. Telling a smoker that they can't smoke is… well, let's just say that it's not a good idea.

One night in particular on an evening that we were sold out of smoking rooms, a business woman came in from a long night of flight delays and meetings all afternoon. It was near midnight, and all she wanted was a comfortable bed, a 6 a.m. wake-up call, and a cigarette. Then it happened. The front desk agent said, "I'm sorry, but we're all sold out of smoking rooms."

This tired, jet-lagged woman suddenly went into a frenzy! After twenty minutes of back-and-forth verbal exchanges and the desk agent virtually offering the "run of the house" to please this woman, the woman said, "This won't do."

Now completely frustrated and at the end of her patience, the desk agent walked over to the hotel lounge and took an ashtray off of the bar and walked back to the front desk and put the ashtray in the woman's hand and said, "Now it's a smoking room!"

Shenanigans

We had a brand new bellman, a youngish African American, and I'll just call him Hank. He was I'd say in his early 30's. He was a great bellman, very professional, proficient, and all of the guests seemed to be quite pleased with him. He asked a lot of questions, which is a good thing.

Then after his two-week training period was up, he was permanently assigned to the graveyard shift. Now on graveyard shifts, staff end up having a lot of downtime. Usually from about 2 a.m. till 5 or 5:30 a.m., it's during that time that people on the graveyard shift start fighting off the urge to find a quiet spot to go to sleep. So they get creative on finding ways to stay awake. Sometimes it is changing the lobby music to something more upbeat and turning up the volume. Sometimes it is raiding the kitchen for room service trays or cooking up a concoction. Sometimes it is exploring the hotel's gym, pool, or helicopter landing pad and taking in the miraculous view of the city from up there. The list of possibilities is endless when thinking about it. However, Hank was more interested in the status of vacant rooms. An odd question for a bellman because vacant room information is strictly for night security and housekeeping.

At any rate, one night Hank asked me to give him a list of vacant and dirty rooms. I asked him why he wanted to know this, as bellman, housekeeping, and security all carried master keys to all of the rooms. He said there was no particular reason that he wanted this information, so I naïvely gave him a list of the rooms that he had asked about. He then disappeared into the night.

It was about 3 a.m. now and we were showing that every reservation for that day had been checked in and accounted for. The phone rang at the front desk, and I noticed it was coming from a room that was listed as vacant. I was naturally curious.

When I answered the phone I recognized Hank's voice on the other end of the line. I asked Hank what he was doing in an unoccupied room, to which he replied that a woman would be coming to the front desk and when she asked for him, he wanted me to direct her to that room.

I said, "Hank you aren't supposed to be in that room! You could get into big trouble."

"He said, "Just do this for me. I'll explain later," and then he hung up. About ten minutes went by and an old beat-up Datsun 280 ZX pulled into the valet parking area. The lady, who was dressed like a common street walker, stepped out of it. The valet told me later that the car was overflowing with garbage and mostly fast-food wrappers and empty plastic bottles. Anyhow, the woman approached the front desk and asked for room 327. I explained to the lady that room 327 was an unoccupied room. She insisted that she was to meet a guy named Hank in room 327! I called the room and Hank answered. I heard hip hop music in the background. He said, "Send her up."

I told Hank that by using the phone in that room he had activated a security alarm in the security office and that the security officer was on his way to investigate. The woman was starting to cause a scene in the lobby, and I was too busy to deal with it so I told her to go on ahead. I'd just let security handle it.

About ten minutes went by and I called the room again, and I told Hank to get the hell out of that room because security was on their way! Well, it was too late. Security had caught him red-handed. Hank was buying drugs from the woman who happened to be a transsexual hooker! Only thing is that Hank didn't know that the she was actually a he! And when they started to get down to business and she whipped out her trouser snake, Hank flipped out! The woman ran from the room, through the lobby, and demanded her car be brought up immediately! When the Valet asked for the parking fee, she caused another scene. I walked out there and told the valet to just let her go.

So there we had it: a drug deal and a hooker in a vacant room, all totally against hotel policy. It pained me to have to do it, but I had to fire Hank on the spot. Employees have gotten away with so much worse, but they knew how to keep it under the radar. Nothing about Hank's little arrangement was under the radar at all. And the fact that he was a relatively new employee meant that he hadn't gained the trust of any of the older employees to cover his ass if needed. Yes, this was an odd night indeed.

No Sleep till Brooklyn

The twelve-story hotel was on a small lot in Beverly Hills and directly faced a three-story shopping mall right across the street. This created a city canyon between us, and all the heavy traffic that went past us and between us was always amplified by the canyon effect. During the day it was no problem because people were awake and keeping themselves busy. Later on in the evening, the traffic died down and people were able to get a good night's rest. Then the routine changed.

One night about 2:30 a.m. an ear-shattering noise lit up the night! It seemed that the mall management had hired a crew to pressure wash the sidewalks out in front of the mall; and for whatever reasons, they chose to do the washing in the wee hours of the morning. I guess so that they wouldn't inconvenience their customers who might get splashed by the water as they were walking into and out of the mall. And because we had that canyon effect, the noise from the gas-powered generator as well as the noise from the high-pressure water hitting the sidewalk was deafening. I started to field several calls from guests who were awakened by the noise.

The only thing I could think to do was to send my security officer out there to talk to the man and see if he could maybe wash the other end of the mall or just turn his generator off completely. The man said, "No." He was given a job to do and he was going to finish it, and he continued to clean the sidewalk for about two hours.

Meanwhile I'm fielding about a dozen calls from guests asking me to stop that noise. And there was basically nothing I could do but to offer them a discount on their bills for the inconvenience.

This got to be a routine event every Sunday night at 2 a.m. for two-plus hours! I finally got the idea to send the cops out there to deal with them. After all, there's a city ordinance that basically says that people cannot make disturbing or nuisance noises after 10 p.m. at night and before 8 a.m. in the morning. So I was hoping that the LAPD would hit the guy with this information and issue a citation, which would give him an incentive to stop working. No dice! The guy was not having any of it, and we were at a loss of what to do about it. And we were losing revenue due to making adjustments on our guests' bills for the inconvenience every week.

Finally our management talked to their management and let them know about the ongoing problem. But the mall management didn't seem to be too responsive to our simple request. After all, they could wash the sidewalks during the day or at least between 7 p.m. and 10 p.m. after the mall closed, and that would solve both of our problems and would be a happy compromise. Still no dice. After working with them and being very personable and professional, we finally had to take legal action. It's not the avenue that we wanted to pursue but the mall management wasn't giving us too many other choices.

Three months had passed of this every-Sunday-night fight, and thankfully the judge ruled in our favor citing the city noise ordinance.

The hotel staff wanted their guests to have an enjoyable stay and were willing to do whatever it took to please them—because they wanted them to come back again and again.

Damage Incorporated

Damage to a guest's belongings by the hotel staff is actually somewhat of a rare occurrence, but it does happen. Ms. Halinski had been a guest at another hotel, and they had damaged a recoiling strap that had a hook on it to keep the suitcase closed. The other hotel did a haphazard repair on the bag. They didn't even send it out to a certified repair shop; they just "mickey moused" it together.

Well, Ms. Halinski had made it over to my hotel; and now in a different city we found ourselves dealing with her problem. For whatever reason, Ms. Halinski had asked us to store her luggage. She gave her bag to me but failed to inform me of the damage to her luggage by the other hotel. The next day when she came to claim her bag, for some reason the bag wouldn't close, and furthermore, the locking mechanism on the side of the bag appeared to have been broken. And the chop job that the other hotel had done was that they had put the hook on the recoiling strap on backwards.

Ms. Halinski was obviously upset about this turn of events. She blamed me personally for damaging her luggage. I found out through other sources that her luggage had been damaged elsewhere (the recoiling strap), but nonetheless she was demanding that I/we take responsibility for the repairs. She said that she was on her way to San Francisco, and as soon as her bag was repaired that we should send the bag to her there.

I can say that I did not cause the further damage to her bag as she had claimed, and I thought that the prior hotel was the one that should be footing the bill for Ms. Halinski's luggage. Unfortunately, we were never able to neither prove nor disprove anything, so out of courtesy to Ms. Halinski we sent her luggage out to a certified Samsonite repair shop, and we paid to have her luggage shipped to her next destination. All is well that ends well.

The hotel did not mind taking responsibility for damage to the guest's item. Of course we were always very careful to not cause damage to anyone's belongings, but it happened from time to time. And remember, we were making upwards of $30,000 a night in revenue so a minor repair on a piece of luggage wasn't going to hurt us financially.

Frequent Fliers

Hotel staff is willing to do just about anything to get repeat business and have their guests recommend their hotel to their friends. As such there are some really good deals to be had when knowing how to ask about them. Usually when a prospective guest calls a hotel, the first rate that they throw out is what we refer to as the rack rate, meaning that is the highest possible rate a guest will pay as a walk-in without a reservation who doesn't have some sort of discount card (AAA, AARP, etc.) or doesn't belong to a company that has negotiated a lower rate with us. Additionally, with the rise in internet travel sites such as Hotwire and Expedia, which have the absolute rock-bottom rates negotiated with the hotels, booking through one of those sites results in getting the best deal. The only other better deal on rates is for a hotel employee or an employee's family member staying for a night or two.

Just as an example, the hotel where I was working was rated 4 stars and was pretty snazzy. It had a rack rate of $289.00 a night (which was years ago; it would be higher now). For guests with some sort of a discount card (AARP, AAA, etc.), the rate dropped to $175.00 a night. Pretty good so far. That rate also went for large groups of people like wedding parties and family reunions. Still a good deal. Then there were companies with their employees who did a lot of traveling, and their rate was anywhere from $89.00 to $150.00 a night, depending on how often they stayed and how many rooms they reserved. Then there was the internet rate of $75.00 to $89.00 for those who prepaid their rooms through a website like Hotel.com and used their discount!

It is just like I have a few friends who are flight attendants, and they are able to get me some great deals on airfares. It's called "You scratch my back and I'll scratch yours!"

Air Drops

There are times when a major airline has had to cancel flights for whatever reasons, but usually it's mechanical malfunctions or bad weather. And if it happens on a late-night flight, then the airlines staff suddenly find themselves needing to put up a planeload of passengers overnight or else they would have 200 people sleeping in the airport lounge. Anyone who has ever done a lot of flying has probably had or probably will experience this at some point in time. Then the airlines find themselves dealing with 200 angry and frustrated passengers! That's when the call goes out to the big hotels with 200 to 1,000 rooms. It's what we refer to in the hotel business as an "air drop."

The call comes into the front desk and the airline in question asks us if we have 200 rooms available at midnight. They want to pay for the room night and breakfast. They will also need shuttle service to and from the airport for all of the passengers. Now by 11:30 p.m. the regular swing shift is already gone, and it's just a skeleton crew of graveyard employees who suddenly find themselves dealing with a few hundred people! That's when things get really crazy and really stressful!

As soon as the call comes in, we have to gather together 200 room keys and 200 individual vouchers for the hotel restaurant meals. We forego the filling out of the registration cards because we just don't have that kind of time in dealing with so many people in the middle of the night. We do, however, ask for credit cards to take care of any other incidental charges that are not being covered by the airlines.

Less than 30 minutes after the airline calls, the shuttles start arriving with the distressed passengers. They line up at the front desk, and we just start handing them keys and vouchers and quickly swipe credit cards and get them up to their rooms in a timely and orderly fashion. It's extremely fast-paced, especially when only one or two front desk agents are on at that time of the night. It happens a lot and we are prepared and thoroughly versed in everything that needs to be done to ensure a seamless process.

I'm not lying when I say that the adrenaline is pumping and the blood pressure is topping out because we've still got audit deadlines to make as well. But within an hour, all 200 passengers are checked in and tucked in.

Conversely, there are stragglers that get bumped off of their flights because they were on "stand by" and the flight was overbooked. Those folks don't get the luxury of having the airlines pay for their rooms, but they do offer them a travel voucher to bring to the hotel, which allows them to stay at a rate of $35.00 per night in a four-star hotel. (See Appendix for advice if this happens to you.)

There are smaller air drops as well, some as small as a dozen passengers all the way up to a few hundred passengers. It's all in a night's work, and we're usually on such a high and giving each other high fives after all is said and done.

Policies and Procedures

I've worked in several four-star hotels in and around the Los Angeles area in hotels that had anywhere from 500 to 1,000 rooms, and I've always worked as a night auditor. When I was in Beverly Hills, I was expected to operate as a night manager without the actual title or pay associated with said title. I was expected to handle everything that was thrown at me in a productive, proactive, professional and democratic way; and of this I assure you I always did. Although I wanted the official title, it always remained just out of my reach because I don't have a college degree. That simple little piece of paper always seemed to hold me back. I didn't really mind because I enjoyed the work that I did and I actually had fun at work. However, sometimes I did have a rough night. It just goes with the territory, as evidenced in the following heart-felt plea to management.

"It is very stressful working on the graveyard shift, and I am expected to be auditor, manager, front desk agent, PBX, reservationist, room service attendant, and bellman. I have to have specialized knowledge and have been cross trained in many different areas to be a fully functional and fully capable member of the hotel staff. The graveyard does not get many opportunities to be rewarded for their efforts. Nor do we have the support of the rest of the hotel at our disposal, such as technical services, engineers etc. I have been empowered to make my own judgement calls when necessary, and I am confident that management will stand behind my decisions.

Sometimes a bad judgement call is made or a stressful evening or situation can cause a temporary clouding of the mind causing an embarrassing or awkward moment for the hotel and the guest. Mistakes happen but never with malicious intent. I do the best I can with what I've got. It is my every intention to elevate the reputation of the hotel to the highest standards in the eyes of the guests and management. I pledge to do whatever is called upon me to be done.

"The hotels that I've worked for all ran a pretty tight ship. The lines of communication were open and things got done in a timely fashion. However, this hotel is different. I've always worked for American companies, and this is my first adventure with a French-owned company. It's obvious that the French have a much different approach to management than the United States does. So I have been feeling frustrated. I feel like there is no structure, no guidelines, and no boundaries. I feel that no one really appreciates the work of the night auditors, and I haven't been real clear on how to resolve these issues.

"Telling multiple department heads about things that happen on the graveyard shift through word-of-mouth only is like playing that childhood game called "Post Office" where someone starts at the front of the line by saying, "Have a good day" and by the time the message gets down to the last person in the line, "Have a good day" becomes "Have the trash taken out at midnight!" The message just gets misconstrued and twisted as everyone puts their own spin on the story. So being proactive as I am, I implemented a new procedure of writing out a nightly report, making several copies, and making sure to deliver it to all of the department heads before I clocked out and went home."

It went over well and management was happy that I was thinking outside of the box. Since the majority of the work that is done on the night audit goes to the accounting department each day, and since the hotel had just put a brand new computer operating system into place and we were all trying to learn it, accounting started getting into nitpicking wars done entirely through memos. There were many unnecessary and accusatory memos, which only bogged down the night audit with having to read them all with limited time to perform our nightly functions. Well, it all came to a head one night as Andre, my co-auditor, wrote this response to a slew of memos from accounting:

"We have to wonder if the accounting department understands how to research information in the new system. You can easily see through our simple layout of information obtained from the new system, with less than five minutes of research, how the facts represent themselves.

"We work very hard each and every night to meet the standards set forth by the accounting department, to not only meet but to exceed the standard each and every day, to be proactive and challenge obstacles and question inaccuracies. We strive for excellence!

"We are doing our best to understand the new system in a night audit sense, and it really undermines the morale of the night audit staff and obstructs the functions of the night audit when the accounting department points the finger of blame without thoroughly investigating the circumstances.

"For example, many of the PERMISSIONS to run the new system were taken away from the night audit staff several weeks ago. The system field technician was here on a follow-up visit as a direct result of the accounting department's finger-pointing tactics. If the field technician had not been with us that night, the night audit could not have been run! The field technician restored our MINIMAL PERMISSIONS; and since then, every night has brought us new and interesting challenges that require a high level of creativity to accomplish the audit. It would be nice to have ALL of our PERMISSIONS restored so that we could focus more attention on a higher level of guest service and a higher quality of night audit and spend less time writing these lengthy memos!"

Your Car, Sir

We had another big foray in a large banquet room; the hotel was advertising it as a "Casino Night" in the city. The place was hopping, and the valet parking attendants were quite busy. However, one gentleman was leaving the party and asked for his car to be brought up. He waited rather patiently for more than ten minutes just thinking that the valets were extremely busy. At some point the man inquired about his vehicle, again saying that he was tired and needed to get home. The valet came back with a small problem. They couldn't find this gentleman's keys! They had been looking everywhere; they had even backtracked through the entire parking area thinking that they may have dropped the keys somewhere. The guest was getting irritated, and so André, the night auditor, was called in to help search for this man's keys. There were two valets, André, two bellmen, and a night houseman all looking for those keys. They searched for well over two hours and came up empty- handed.

The gentleman was understandably upset because he said that ALL of his keys were on that key ring. We offered to give the gentleman a free night's stay in our hotel that night, or if he would like, we would gladly pay for his cab ride home. He made a phone call and was able to wake one of his roommates up so he opted for the free cab ride.

We never did find that man's keys, and ultimately we had to pay to replace every key on the key ring including his car key. The valet parking attendants were not actually employees of the hotel. They were hired by an outside agency, but they still represented our hotel. It was after that evening debacle that it was suggested that the valet parking attendants be trained in proper guest service for future encounters.

ATM Trouble

Most hotels, and most businesses for that matter, have resorted to placing ATM machines for their customers' convenience. Yes, they charge an outlandish fee, but people pay for the convenience.

One particular night, the ATM was unusually busy; and in a short time, it ran out of money. One guest, who was attending a function in one of our banquet rooms, was trying to get cash for a cab ride home. It is in those incidents that the hotel can still comfortably accommodate guests. We have two avenues from which to choose. We can either issue a taxi cab voucher and pay for the cab ride or authorize a credit card for up to $100.00 and then issue a "pay out" to the hotel cashier and give the person the money.

It's not that big of a deal, but a lot of people don't know to ask about that service; and it's not general knowledge that we do that for our valued guests. Remember, the guest comes first and the customer is always right. No one should be afraid to ask if and how a hotel can help them out when in a tough spot.

Human GPS

So I'm kind of famous for my navigation skills. I've lived in Los Angeles most of my life, and I've intimately explored every inch of this wonderful city by bus, rail, and car. I really know my way around. When I was a teenager, my stepfather was a long-haul truck driver; and on summer breaks from school, I would go on the road with him, so I became very adept at reading maps and finding landmarks.

Guests want to know the best eateries, best sights to see, and they like to find those out-of-the-way places that only the locals know about, and I always had a lot of guests asking me how to get there. Trying to explain how to get there can be problematic for many reasons, up to and including the language barrier. The best way that I could help was to draw them a map! Therefore, a map-making career was started. I'd whip out my pen and paper and lay down the lines, marking the major streets with names, and putting little directional arrows and "X's" that marked off landmarks. I made the maps as simple as possible.

Sometimes I would catch a phone call at the front desk from a guest needing directions to the hotel from the LAX airport or some other location. They were usually in a panic because they were in a big city in the middle of the night and didn't want to make a wrong turn into a seedy area of town. I always spoke calmly and professionally and gained their confidence with my own confidence in my knowledge of the city.

One night a guest called me from his tour bus. He said he was bringing the band the "B 52's" to my hotel, and he was about

30 miles away and several freeways were closed off on his route, and he didn't know which way to go to get to the hotel.

I said, "No problem." I knew about the freeway closures and I also knew the backroads. I took him off the freeway and onto surface streets to get around the closures, and then I got him back onto the freeway as he got closer to the hotel. I stayed on the phone with him the entire time to keep him calm and get him and the band here safely.

When the band finally arrived, the driver was so impressed with me that he told me that he was actually the owner of the charter bus company; and he said that if I ever got my CDL (Commercial Driver's License) I have a job anytime!

It is nights like that that really made my job worthwhile.

What's Actually Normal?

There are many people from all parts of the world; and believe it or not, everything is not standard like it is in the United States, such as we all run on standard 110-volt electricity so our wall outlets are designed for just that. However, European countries are standard 220-volt systems; and therefore their electric appliances will not work or even fit into our standard 110 outlets. They need a special adapter to run their hair dryers, curling irons, and what not; and hotels usually have a very limited number of adapter kits on hand at the front desk or via the housekeeping department. Although Europe has standard 220-volt systems, the wall outlets change design from country to country; so there's about five to seven different outlet configurations, and we usually have all of them in our kits.

Another thing foreign guests typically ask is how to turn on the water in the bathtub, how to flush the toilets, how to turn on the lights, and how to use the pay phones. I've often wondered what could be so hard about doing these simple, ordinary tasks. You'd be surprised at how often we are asked these questions.

Then I myself traveled to Europe and spent significant time in nine different countries. My main stops were first England and France and then Italy and Germany.

I arrived in London at the Heathrow airport, and I immediately went to find a pay phone so I could call my brother, who was living in Germany at the time. I found the pay phone and to my complete surprise, I didn't see where the coins went in. I looked for two or three minutes and I felt stupid! How can I not know how to use a pay phone? I finally asked a passerby, and he was very helpful. That afternoon I arrived in my hotel room and went to use the restroom; I wanted to take a relaxing shower after my long flight from New York. And then another surprise! I couldn't figure out how to flush the toilet or how to turn on the shower! The bathroom fixtures were completely different from anything that I'd ever seen before. Believe it or not, every single country that I went to, I found myself having to ask how to use the pay phone, toilet, and shower. The designs were completely different in every country. I didn't bring any electric appliances so I didn't have to ask for their adapter kits, but I did take note of the different wall outlet designs, all different.

I found other odd occurrences in Europe as well: They don't have ice cubes, which is a staple here in the United States. They don't have a vast selection of salad dressings like we have here; what you get is two bottles, one with oil and the other with vinegar, that are standardly placed on your dining table along with the salt and pepper. And as my brother so keenly pointed out to me, there are no doorknobs in Europe! Everything is a "handle".

Ever since my trip abroad I have much more sympathy and understanding for foreign travelers. Because what's every day and normal in America is NOT every day and normal around the world.

Chapter 5: The Language Barrier

Speak English or Die

Every day we were dealing with people from all over the world, people that speak other languages, and people that try hard but speak in broken English because they haven't mastered it yet or they are just passing through the United States on their holiday. We did our best to find and hire a wide range of employees who also spoke many different languages to pitch in and to help when needed. I tried really hard to understand what they were getting at and to get them what they needed. Sometimes it came across using both sign language and bits of broken English. I had guests show me maps and tourist pamphlets and fliers to get their messages across. We did whatever it took.

Sometimes we got rude or inconsiderate guests or guests who were just trying to be funny to get a reaction out of their traveling companions. They would ask rude or distasteful questions in their native tongues, knowing that we wouldn't understand what they were saying. But we could generally tell when we were being insulted in a foreign langue just by their friends' reactions.

I had one such encounter with a male flight attendant from Mexicana Airlines. He came in with about five other female flight attendants, and while I was getting them their room keys and daily per diems, the male flight attendant looked me square in the face and said, "Te quiero pisarle." All of the girls immediately looked shocked, and their faces turned red as they were covering their faces with their hands in embarrassment. The male just smiled a great big smile and batted his eyes at me. I didn't know what he had said to me, but I knew it wasn't good.

So before I handed him his room key I stepped into the back office real quick and called out to my coworker Ingrid, who was Guatemalan and I said, "Ingrid, Te quiero pisarle," and she immediately gasped! I said, "This flight attendant from Mexicana Airlines just said that to me. What does it mean?"

Ingrid said that it depends on where you're from. In some places it is rooster or barnyard talk meaning "I want to step on you," but in other places it means "I want to fuck you."

I said, "Oh, okay, thanks Ingrid."

I went back out to the front desk and put a smile on my face, and then I changed his room assignment, which had been pre-blocked earlier in the day to make sure that the flight crew all stayed together as per the contract with the airline.

But I put him on the third floor, which basically had all small meeting rooms that could be converted to extra rooms if the need arises. Those rooms all had Murphy Beds (the kind of old-fashion beds that pull out and away from the inside of the wall). He also got the room nearest to the service elevator and ice machine, virtually ensuring a sleep-deprived night.

I also filed a formal complaint with his employer the next day. Hopefully that taught that guy a lesson. I don't know if he ever got reprimanded or if he lost his job. But oddly enough, I never saw him again with any regular airline crews. It pays to be nice to the front desk agents!

The Saudi Royals

One day we were told that a royal family from Saudi Arabia would be staying with us for an extended period of time. We were told to NEVER ask them for any form of payment, and we were to give them anything that they asked for. In other words they were completely free to, pardon the pun, royally fuck us over!

The day that they checked in, they presented us with a personal check, drawn on a U.S. bank, in the minuscule amount of $2,000, of which we were told NOT to deposit. They arrived with an entourage of family and personal servants; and they were not dressed like Saudi royals in headbands and togas, but in regular western United States garb. They didn't even approach the front desk. One of our day managers walked out to the lobby and presented their room keys to them. Twelve rooms in all and all on the highest floor and two suites. Now rack rate at that hotel was $289.00 a night and the suites ran upwards of $700.00 a night. That's about $4,800 for the first night alone, because if I remember correctly the royals weren't getting any kind of discount rates. So that initial $2,000 wasn't going to cover that first night, let alone a 30-day stay; and as a night auditor who watches the hotels bottom line every day, well that just didn't sit well with me at all.

Most four-star hotels have safety deposit boxes for their guests' convenience. At this particular hotel, policy would dictate that an employee stay with a guest while they conducted their business at a safety deposit box. In other words, we got to see exactly what guests were putting into their boxes and taking out of their boxes. We had to keep totally anonymity, of course. The king or sheik (or whatever you want to call him) stepped in and filled his safety deposit box with rolls of U.S. $100 bills wrapped with rubber bands. His wife and teenage son also filled their own boxes with rolls of hundreds. They came down every day, sometimes twice a day, to grab a few hundreds before going out in the town.

We offer a faxing service for $2.00 per page for incoming as well as outgoing faxes, and every single morning around 5 a.m., they would send out a fax to their bank in Saudi Arabia asking to wire transfer money into their U.S. accounts. Now, have any of you that are reading this story so far have any bells going off? Or see red flags anywhere?

That was just the beginning of the chaos that they would bring down upon us. We were NOT allowed to ask for a credit card to cover incidentals, such as pay-per-view movies, phone calls, valet parking, and minibar charges. I argued this point vehemently with my superiors, but I was told in no uncertain terms, "Leave the royals alone."

It started off with the sheik's son rollerblading through the lobby on a daily basis after being told each time that such an activity was prohibited in the building for safety reasons. He then went into the hotel gift shop and tried to buy a pack of cigarettes, which of course we couldn't do because state law says you've got to be at least 18 years old to purchase cigarettes. Undeterred, he instead purchased a box of twelve condoms. Less than an hour later he was filling the condoms with water, making water balloons, and he proceeded to drop the water balloons on guests as they pulled into the valet parking area! He nailed one guest in a convertible who happened to be wearing a very expensive Armani suit. Needless to say we got read the riot act from that guest, and we ended up having to pay for his suit and have his car detailed.

I guess the hotel had a design flaw in that the windows opened and didn't have screens on them.

A few nights later the sheik's son was on the other side of the hotel facing the hotel loading zone. He was dropping silverware and empty champagne bottles out of the window trying to hit the employees that were out there on cigarette breaks. We sent hotel security upstairs to deal with him.

One night his son called down to the front desk to ask us to unblock his adult movies. I said, "I'm sorry but your father said specifically not to do that." He tried to tell me that it wasn't for him, that his grandfather wanted to watch a movie.

I said, "Put your grandfather on the phone and have him tell me himself." The boy told me that his grandfather didn't speak English.

I said, "Then have your father talk to me personally when he gets back; if it's okay with him, then I'll do it." The boy got angry, said a few choice words, and hung up.

One night he came down to the lobby and got into a screaming match with my relief auditor, Giovani. As he approached the front desk, Giovani was so riled up that he jumped over the front desk and grabbed the sheik's son by the shirt collar and started to swing on him! I jumped over the front desk and grabbed Giovani's arm and held him back! I said, "Gio! Back office—now!"

Gio went into the back office, and I went into damage-control mode and profusely apologized to the sheik's son and did my best to ensure that he wouldn't let this incident get back to his father. What a huge lawsuit that would have been!

I went back into the back office and chewed Gio out. I said, "I know that kid is a fucking nuisance, and we're all tired of dealing with the little shit, but what in the ever-living hell were you thinking? He's not worth losing your job over."

After that night the kid pretty much kept his nose clean for the rest of his family's stay. Thank God for small favors.

My Uncle Manuel lived and worked in Saudi Arabia for 30 years, so I knew a lot about their laws and culture. For one thing, alcohol is illegal in Saudi Arabia. Suffice it to say, my uncle was always drunk the minute he got off the plane in the U.S. and stayed drunk until the minute he got back on the plane to Saudi. But that's a different story.

The reason I mention this is because the sheik's wife called room service and asked for a Margarita one afternoon. When the attendant got to her door he said, "Here's your drink," to which she asked, "Is their alcohol in it?" The attendant said "Yes" to which she replied, "Then take it away; I don't want it!"

This same routine went on about three times in a row, and I got a call at the front desk by an extremely frustrated room service attendant. He said, "She keeps asking if it has alcohol in it, and of course it does! Talk to the lady and find out what her "trip" is?"

About the time I got off the phone with the attendant, I got another call from the sheik's wife, and she was whispering so low that I could barely hear her. She said, "Alcohol is illegal in my country. I want alcohol in my drink, but my husband is here, and he can't know about it; so when I ask if it has alcohol in it, tell the attendant to say NO!"

I replied "So you're basically going to lie to your husband?"

And she answered, "Yes."

I called Room Service and explained the situation. He was relieved and took the sheik's wife her Margarita and told her, "No alcohol in it" when he got there. He called me later and we had a good laugh over it.

One fine evening about 1 a.m. in the morning, the sheik came into the lobby from the valet parking area; and on his arm was a beautiful six-foot-tall blonde. She could have been a Playboy or Penthouse model; she was that beautiful. They were laughing and carrying on, and the sheik approached me at the front desk and asked for another room. So I gave him one, and before he left the desk he said, "And don't tell my wife about it." I just chuckled under my breath and went on about my business.

About an hour later, around 2 a.m., the sheik's wife also came strolling through the lobby with her own tall, dark, and handsome man on her arm. They were also laughing and carrying on. She approached the desk, and she also asked for another room. She added, "And don't tell my husband." All of us on duty that night had one hell of a good laugh about that. I guess the Las Vegas saying holds true no matter where you are? "What happens in Los Angeles stays in Los Angeles."

Meanwhile the royal family has been in our hotel for almost 30 days at rack rate and with absolutely no form of payment on file except for that initial check for $2,000 that we still had not yet deposited. They were faxing their bank every day, had parked five cars every day, and were racking up charges in the restaurant, making phone calls, and raiding their minibars. I was watching these charges add up every night and not being able to balance the books each night because of the lack of payment on record. I had voiced my concerns several times to management and accounting and each time I was asked to, "Stand down."

I said "Okay, but these guys probably aren't even really royals and they're probably running one hell of a scam on us!"

Their final night with us was unusual in the fact that they all assembled in the lobby and asked for their cars to be brought up at 2 a.m. in the morning when check out time was 11 a.m. They had all their luggage with them.

I asked them if they were checking out, and the sheik said, "No, we are not checking out." As soon as all their cars were brought up, they all climbed in and drove off into the night.

When the morning crew arrived at 6 a.m., I informed them of what had happened a few hours earlier and that they hadn't come back. My manager dispatched housekeeping to their rooms; and to our utter shock (not mine), they found that not only had they left the hotel but that they had also taken everything that wasn't nailed down! We're talking robes, towels, bedding, lamps, coffee makers, mirrors that were hanging on the walls—you name it—and they left with it! And surprise, surprise… their check for $2,000 bounced! That supposed royal family left us owing over $200,000. And there was absolutely no paper trail to go after them because they hadn't even filled out a single registration card. Now that's one hell of a scam in my opinion. Next time I need a room, I'm just going to tell them that I'm royalty!

Moshi Moshi

It was an early Tuesday morning in the wee hours of the day before 5 a.m. The lobby was quiet, silence broken only by the sound of the front desk phone. A quick glance indicated that the call was coming from outside of the hotel. So as I picked up the receiver I knew that I had to say, "Bonjour, this is the hotel; how may I direct your call?"

The first sound that I heard was an Asian man's voice, "Moshi-moshi. I Japanese, moshi-moshi." The words moshi-moshi pierced together like rounds from an automatic weapon. Moshi-moshi, means "hello" in Japanese. Then ever so carefully, each word thereafter selected and spoken ever so slowly sounded as if the man had an English dictionary that he was trying his best to use, with a loud pausing sigh in between each word. Sounding something like this: "Aye Japanese…yeah…I go shopping at Beverly Cent-ah…yeah…and I walk to your hotel, and I uhm, ask for taxi cab. Man at door introduce me to his friend. He take me to my hotel, and he charge me four-tee doll-ah. Seems expensive—yes?"

Listening carefully and trying to decipher his message through his thick Japanese accent, I stood bewildered by his statement. Fourteen dollars seemed reasonable to me for a cab ride in Los Angeles. But what about the friend of the doorman? Who was this friend that he was introduced to? It didn't sound like he got a taxi; it sounded more like a friend of the doorman's took him home and charged him $14.00. If that were the case, then we were looking at a whole new situation that could have potentially bad results both for the hotel and the doorman.

So now with my Japanese vocabulary being limited to only what I can order on a Japanese restaurant menu, I had to try and piece this mystery together to solve a problem. I replied to the man on the phone slowly so he would have a better chance of understanding my English.

"Do-you-want-to-speak-to-a-manager?"
"Do-you-want-to-make-a-complaint?"

"Do-you-want-to-talk-to-the-boss?"

And silently to myself I continued the thought process: big cheese? Head honcho? Number-one man? The man continued "Last time in LA, cab driver charge me twenty doll-ah. This time he charge four-tee doll-ah. Seems expensive—yes?"

Suddenly it all made sense! He said $40.00, not $14.00. Well, yeah, that was definitely no bargain-base cab ride! This guy got ripped off! Okay, but now I still have the problem of who gave him this expensive ride.

As I'm trying to put a game plan together, I see an Asian looking woman walking through my lobby. Light bulb goes off in my head. I said to the woman, "Excuse me." She turned and looked at me and then I motioned for her to approach me. She came over to the desk and I asked her "Do you speak Japanese?"

She smiled excitedly like she had just won a prize or something. The Japanese all seem to be pretty excitable anyway. She said "Yes, Moshi-moshi," and then I asked her, "Would you speak to this man on the telephone for me and find out what he wants?"

She said, "Yes, I will talk to him." She also had a very heavy Asian accent. She picked up the phone and said, "Moshi-moshi" and continued conversing for several minutes. Then she paused and said to me, "He say he pay $40.00 dollar for a taxi and that seems expensive."

I said "Ask him if he would like to file a complaint with our manager?"

She spoke to him again and said, "No, he just want to tell you that it seems expensive for a taxi cab."

Now my mind is wandering again. He's calling a hotel in Los Angeles at around 4:50 a.m. in the morning just to tell me that it seems expensive for a $40.00 cab ride? What is he thinking? So in my bewilderment I said to the woman, "Tell him that this hotel does not own the taxi cab company. They come here out of courtesy for our guests." And then I added, "Does he remember the name of the taxi cab that he got into?"

The woman relayed the message and then she said, "He say he take big black taxi cab."

I'm thinking big black taxi cab; we don't have any big black taxi cabs. All our cabs are yellow and a few blues, but no blacks. Then I'm searching my memory banks and I think, big black taxi cab? That sounds like a limo? I said to the woman "You mean he took a ride in a limousine?"

She chattered back to him and smiled. The smile turned into a chuckle and she said, "Yes, he took a ride in a limousine."

And I said, "Well, there you have it! Mystery solved! A limo ride is definitely going to cost $40.00."

She spoke one last time and then in almost perfect sync we both realized the hilariousness of the situation and the embarrassment the man must have felt at that moment as we both broke into laughter. The woman hung up the phone and I thanked her for her assistance and she was still laughing as she walked away.

Chop Suey

One particular night I had a small regiment of Japanese businessmen check into the hotel. They had apparently all had an awful day of traveling: late/missed connections, lost luggage, slow shuttle service, and nothing to eat all day. When they finally arrived at our hotel, they were understandably irritated and upset. However, they chose to take it out on the front desk agents at the hotel. I was checking them in, and they obviously had little knowledge of the English language, so I was having trouble understanding them to pull up their reservations.

Suddenly three of the gentleman in the group became very animated. It seemed to me that they were also frustrated by the lack of communication. They started yelling at me in Japanese, and all I could do was take it! I found some Japanese names on the incoming reservations list, so I was asking for their passports in order to confirm that that was them and get them checked into their rooms. They were still yelling at me.

About that time Andre, my co-auditor, came out from the back office because he had overheard the scuttlebutt and wanted to see if he could help. The Japanese business men were in high gear about that time, and then Andre spoke to them in perfect Japanese! Now Andre is a six-foot-tall African American man who wears glasses, and he's the last person that one would expect would speak perfect Japanese! The businessmen were shocked at his precise command of their language, and they immediately began bowing and apologizing to Andre in their language. Andre finished checking them in, and as they backed away from the front desk, they continued bowing and apologizing.

After they had gone I asked Andre, who had studied Japanese in college and had lived in Japan for two years, what they were saying. Andre said that they were using very foul language and were insulting and belittling me as well as others in the hotel. They were quite surprised to find a Japanese-speaking American, and they were embarrassed and humiliated by their behavior.

Everything turned out okay, but it just goes to show that we should never take any situation for granted. Because we never know who can speak our language.

Just the Fax, Ma'am

Hotel guests can get upset and nitpick about the smallest details. Oftentimes, guests are just very tired and irritable from whatever obstacles their day has thrown at them, and sometimes they are or appear to be under the influence of some sort of alcohol or medication. That's when things get tricky.

Mr. Rubin had a message light on in his room; and when he called down to the front desk, he was told that he had received a fax and he was asked if he wanted it delivered to his room. Mr. Rubin said, "That would be wonderful. Thank you so much!"

Faxes generally come via the PBX department and are logged into a journal, put into an 8" x 11" white envelope, and delivered to the concierge desk until either the guest comes to pick it up themselves or until the bellman delivers it to their rooms. However, on this particular day, the PBX operator had neglected to "turn off" Mr. Rubin's message light. The light had apparently been on and blinking in his room all day, and he never noticed it until the next afternoon.

Mr. Rubin called down to the front desk asking for his messages. Our log book had indicated that he had received a fax the day before and we were debating the issue. I got the strong feeling that he was under the influence of something because of his irrational behavior on the phone and the fact that he seemed to be very confused about the simplest things. Mr. Rubin said that the fax was very important and he needed it for business. I again reiterated the fact that his fax was delivered the previous day. I had even double checked with Alessandro, our concierge on duty that day, and he had assured me that the fax was indeed delivered the day before and there were no new faxes waiting to be delivered. Mr. Rubin was what we refer to as a "tough customer," and he asked for a manager to call him to discuss his apparently missing fax.

Things can really get misconstrued when the hotel drops the ball on something as simple as remembering to turn off a message light after a guest has made contact with the PBX department.

Chapter 6: The Danger Zone

Trapped

In the hotel there is what we call "the front of the house," which is the lobby, gift shop, and restaurants—the parts that all of our guests see. Then there is "the back of the house:" housekeeping department, storage rooms, and the employee cafeteria—the parts that only employees get to see. It's usually a labyrinth of long hallways and service elevators that can be very challenging to memorize to know where we're going. In this particular hotel the employee cafeteria was located in the basement one floor down from the ground floor, and we could only access it from the main service elevator that was behind the front desk.

I had managed to slip away from the front desk for a few minutes at around midnight that night because I was pretty hungry and I needed something to snack on. The ride down was uneventful. However, the ride back up was anything but eventful. I entered the service elevator and pressed the button for the first floor; the doors closed, and I was on my way. However, the elevator had passed the first floor and had stopped on what the indicator light had identified as the third floor. But the elevator doors didn't open at all. I pressed the first-floor button again, and this time the elevator shot up rather quickly and stopped in between floors with a sudden jolt! I tried to manually open the doors but wasn't having any luck, so I used the emergency telephone that was in the elevator to call my supervisor at the front desk to let him know what was going on. My second call was to the engineering department to get me the hell out of there! Now, I'm not claustrophobic in the least bit, but being trapped in an elevator between floors and not knowing when or how I was going to get out was definitely nerve wracking.

Engineering called me up and asked what floor I was on. I said that the LED indicators were saying that I was stuck between the second and third floors. Engineering said that they were on the third floor, and could I hear them knocking on the outer door.

I asked engineering, "Where the hell am I?"

They said that they didn't know and to hold on because they were making their way up to me floor by floor. I could feel the elevator moving slightly but it was moving so slowly that I couldn't tell if I was moving up or down? After about 15 minutes, I finally was able to hear some knocking sounds. I asked if that was them knocking?

They said, "Yes."

I asked them where I was exactly, but they didn't tell me. They just said, "Hold on; we're prying the doors open now." The doors started opening slowly. I saw a crowbar punching through the doors. When they finally got the doors fully opened up, as I looked down I could see just the tops of their heads. So I was obviously still in between floors! There was only about a two-foot gap between the floor of the elevator and the top of the door. The guys got about a five-foot step ladder and propped it up against the elevator floor, and then I had to bend down and crawl out of the elevator backwards. Viola! I was free! And I didn't get a single scratch.

I asked the engineer, "Where exactly are we?"

Then he said, "We're on the twelfth floor."

The hotel only had twelve floors. The elevator had jammed itself up past the twelfth floor and was trying to pop out through the roof!

I said, "Wow, that's just too weird!" I had calmed down and engineering directed me to the guest elevators to get back down to the lobby. But after that little adventure I was too paranoid to get into another elevator so I walked down twelve flights of stairs. Now I'm always weary of any elevator.

Thank you, Drive Thru

Now I'm not like most people you'll meet in that I have some psychic abilities. Ever since I was a child I have received visions of things yet to come. The visions I receive usually come when I'm wide awake, and they play out as short 30-second video clips in my mind's eye, and they repeat over and over again in brief increments, sometimes for three or four days.

One afternoon at work I suddenly got a vision. It was of several men wearing all black, and they were rushing toward me and had shotguns set back against their shoulders, and they were aimed directly at me! This was most certainly a disturbing vision because I immediately thought that maybe the hotel was going to be robbed by several dark-clothed shotgun toting thugs!

I saw the vision for several days as per the usual circumstance. I was very nervous and jumpy for a few days, but I decided not to tell any of my coworkers about my vision for fear that they A) wouldn't believe me or B) they might think I'm crazy if they were close-minded individuals. At any rate, a few days went by and the vision had finally run its course and nothing out of the ordinary had happened so I started to relax a bit.

It was about 3 a.m. in the morning on this particular night. Suddenly in the distance I could hear the sounds of sirens coming from emergency vehicles. The sirens were getting closer and louder by the minute. It sounded like a brigade of vehicles and sirens. I started to wonder what could possibly be happening out there on Century Boulevard. Because the last time that I had heard that many sirens flying by, it was a massive emergency response to a plane crash at the Los Angeles airport LAX. I hadn't heard an explosion or anything like that, but I was worried about it.

I stood at the front desk and leaned forward to try to get a glimpse of the emergency vehicles as they drove by. But something struck me as odd about it because it actually sounded as if they were coming right up our driveway! And as I leaned over and strained to see what was happening, suddenly a convertible sports car came smashing through the set of glass double doors shattering them into thousands of shards. I heard the engine of the car's engine revving up higher and higher as if the driver's foot was on the gas pedal and it was on the floor. The car was headed straight for me so I quickly ran into the back office to escape injury and/or death.

As I closed the door to the back office, I could see the car losing traction on the lobby carpet; and as the driver tried to overcompensate, the car radically fishtailed and turned toward the bell desk that was in front of the guest elevators. I heard a loud bang as if the car had crashed into something, and then I heard the engine cut off. The car didn't collide with the front desk; at least I thought. As I slowly stepped out of the back office, I could see the convertible but I couldn't see the bell desk; and my first thought was, "Oh my God, the bellman is dead!"

Then I noticed a middle-aged man step out of the convertible driver's seat, calmly walk to the elevator, and push the call button, and wait to go up!

I thought, *This isn't happening*. Then as I turned to survey the damage done to the lobby doors, there appeared in the doorway a half a dozen Los Angeles police officers in their dark blue uniforms with shoulder mounted shotguns aiming directly at me as they quickly advanced in my direction. I immediately ducked down behind the front desk to avoid getting caught in the crossfire if it were to come to that. They ran at the driver of the car and gang tackled him as he was calmly waiting for the elevator doors to open.

So there it was! My vision came to life! What I thought was going to be a robbery turned out to be something quite different.

As the officers were taking the perpetrator down, an airport shuttle bus had pulled into the valet parking area and four German tourists got off and stepped up to the desk to check in. Their flight had arrived at LAX at 2:30 a.m. They were tired, didn't speak any English, and didn't seem to have any curiosity at all about what they had just walked into.

After the scene was secured by the police, they came up to the desk to ask us for our surveillance footage of the incident, and they also told us what had started this whole foray. It seems our middle-aged driver had been pulled over by the Highway Patrol on the 710 Long Beach Freeway. The officer was writing up a ticket, and he took off like a bat out of hell as the officer handed him the ticket for his signature. This in turn started a high-speed pursuit down several freeways. Then he exited onto Century Boulevard where he ran a red light and collided with two vehicles in the intersection. He next continued driving down Century where he pulled into our driveway and proceeded to turn our hotel into a drive thru!

My supervisor and I pulled ourselves together and powdered our noses in case a local news crew had been following the chase and wanted to interview witnesses. We waited all night and not a single crew ever showed up to cover the story. So we missed our opportunity for our fifteen minutes of fame. We were a little disappointed about that, but ultimately we were more grateful that no one was killed or injured. The LA Police Department was absolutely stellar in the handling of this case.

9/11

September 11th started out like any other day until the radio interrupted its classic rock programming to announce that at 5:46

a.m., a small commuter plane had crashed into the World Trade Center in New York! I remember quite clearly of instantly feeling anger. Anger that some stupid idiotic weekend pilot flew his plane into a building! I thought, *How could this happen? What was the pilot thinking? And how many people has he injured or killed?* My co-auditor and I listened intently for more detailed information. The music was over and all they were broadcasting was this horrific event, and we were hanging on the reporters' every word while still in disbelief.

At about 7:39 a.m. Pacific Time, the reporter had an update that at 8:46.40 a.m., American Airlines Flight #11, a Boeing 767 carrying 81 passengers and 11 crew members, departed 14 minutes late from Logan International Airport in Boston, bound for Los Angeles International Airport. Five hijackers were aboard. And that was the plane that had hit the World Trade Center and NOT a small commuter plane as was first reported.

Furthermore, at 9:03.00, Flight #175 crashed into the south face of the South Tower (2 WTC) of the World Trade Center.

"Oh my God," we thought! "This was very unusual. What the hell is going on in New York?"

Then the bad news kept coming and at 9:37:46: which is 6:37 Pacific Time, Flight #77 crashed into the western side of The Pentagon and started a violent fire.

The final blow came at 10:03:11: Flight #93 crashed by its hijackers and passengers, due to fighting in the cockpit 80 miles southeast of Pittsburgh in Somerset County, Pennsylvania.

My shift had ended, but I was at a loss of what to do. This was crazy! We all wondered if this was some crazy mass terrorist attack on America. Was this the first strike in a war on the United States? They hit the East Coast. Are there also targets in Los Angeles? Is it even safe to go home? What was happening?

We had an international internship program where employees were hired from abroad to live and work in the hotel for a period of three to six months, to get their feet wet, and to

102

explore careers in the hospitality industry. Some lived in the hotel, and others did not and were afraid to come into work that morning. The day managers had rounded up all of our interns and had asked them all to call home and let their families know that everything was okay and that they were safe at the moment.

Airline crews were also given free long-distance calls to their families as well. Everyone was extending their stays because all flights were being grounded, and the people had no place else to go until this mess was figured out. Additionally my hotel was offering to extend guest stays at no cost to them.

I finally made it home and watched the horror story unfold on the news. The story was on every channel!

And to my total disbelief at 9:59:00, the South Tower of the World Trade Center collapsed, 56 minutes after the impact of Flight #175.

Followed shortly thereafter at 10:28:22, the North Tower of the World Trade Center collapsed 1 hour and 42 minutes after the impact of Flight #11.

The Marriott Hotel, located at the base of the two towers, was also destroyed. The towers were gone!

I was still in a state of disbelief as to what had just happened, but I was proud to be on a team that "stepped up" when the chips were down. We made sure that guests were safe, had a place to stay, and had called their families to let them know that they were okay.

It turned out that, yes, America was under a terrorist attack, but it was limited to the East Coast. I just thank God that it didn't turn into an all-out war on our home soil. Instead, we took the fight to them. We hunted down Saddam Hussein and Osama Bin Laden, and we made them answer for what they had done to America, and the rest of the world for that matter. We, the home of the brave and the land of the free, will never allow violence or war to come to our shores without holding someone accountable for their actions. It just wouldn't be feasible here because almost every household has a gun or guns or some type of weapons. We are prepared!

What a Blast

It was an election night in Los Angeles in November, a local election for Mayor and City Council seats and a few bond and proposition issues. Our hotel sat caddy-corner from a major hospital in Beverly Hills with a Jewish private elementary school behind us and a major shopping mall directly across the street facing our front door. The night was lively and celebrations were happening both in our hotel and at nearby locations.

It seemed to be an ordinary election night in the city, and then a Los Angeles County Sheriffs Officer appeared and approached me at the front desk. He asked for our security guard on duty. When our guard met him in the lobby, the sheriff instructed our officer to close and lock every entrance to our hotel. He further added that no one was to be allowed to either enter or leave the hotel until further notice.

Curious, I asked the Officer what this was all about. The officer then informed me that a suspicious package had been placed at the front gate of the Jewish School and that the bomb squad was in route to investigate. For safety reasons, a six-block area surrounding the hotel was being cordoned off. I immediately started shaking all over because the way the hotel was set up, the Jewish school was just a mere 200 yards away from the hotel's loading dock, and only one wall was separating us from a possible bomb! I had no other recourse but to start praying for a peaceful and uneventful end with no casualties, and I had to come up with some kind of explanation for guests if anyone should ask what was going on.

Sure enough, shortly after locking the hotel up tight, I started fielding phone calls from guests who were trying to get to the hotel but were being stopped at roadblocks. I told them that due to the election night, there was police activity in the area and that I was very sorry for their inconvenience, but the police were not allowing anyone in or out at the moment. I gave them the address of a very good 24-hour diner nearby and asked them if they could wait there until the *all-clear signal* was given.

Guests from upstairs were beginning to call down because the red and blue lights of the emergency vehicles were glaring through their windows. They wanted to know what was going on. I explained that this was an election night, and one of the candidates was being escorted by police to their celebratory location that was nearby the hotel. That's the story that I was spinning, and the guests were buying it lock, stock, and barrel.

As a representative of my hotel, I had a duty to not insight a panic in my guests. I know it was a bald-faced lie that I was telling them; but really, did anyone want to find out that there might be a bomb just outside their window?

About 2 a.m. we had a lobby full of people that wanted to go home because the parties were over, but the sheriff had not given the okay yet. As people started to ask why they couldn't leave the hotel, suddenly there was a loud explosion out behind the hotel. It was so loud that I swear the concussion rattled the building! Everyone in the lobby went into a panic.

"What the Hell was that?" was the question that everyone was asking.

A few minutes later a sheriff's deputy walked into the hotel and said that everything was okay. He said it wasn't a bomb, but they destroyed it just to be on the safe side. The phones lit up like Christmas with inquiries as to the explosion. I just told guests that there was a late-night fireworks display going on because of election night. They were skeptical of my explanation, but they bought it and everything went smoothly for the rest of the night.

That was a powerful place for a bomb if there ever was one. If it had been real and if it had been during the day with a hospital, shopping mall, school, and hotel at ground zero, well it probably wouldn't have ended very well. I'm glad that my prayers were answered that night.

Possible Hostage Situation

At approximately 11:10 p.m. I answered an outside call at the main PBX console. The female calling simply identified herself as "Melissa." She asked if I would send my in-house security officer to Mr. Borman's room, room 1018. She indicated to me that Mr. Borman was holding her female friend hostage in the room. I immediately called Alan in security and relayed the message to him. Moments later Melissa called again and asked to be put through to Mr. Borman's room.

Security Officer Gustavo made a radio transmission to PBX that there was a hostage situation on the tenth floor, and we may need to call the LAPD. The night houseman was in the lobby sweeping and Gustavo's transmission could be heard quite loudly and quite clearly over the houseman's radio as well, which was disturbing as there were several guests being checked into the hotel at the front desk at that time.

I also called Mr. Borman's room and spoke with Mr. Borman. I simply said to the guest, "It is our understanding that your guest would like to leave the hotel property."

Mr. Borman replied, "Yes, she just walked out the door."

I said, "Thank you and have a good evening."

I watched the lobby elevators and I witnessed only one woman leaving the area. Security Officers Alan and Gustavo reported that they had been to Mr. Borman's room and had briefly questioned him about the information that was relayed to the hotel's staff and additionally had asked Mr. Borman if they could search his room to ensure that the situation was indeed under control. Security Officer Alan stated that Mr. Borman had agreed to the search but was rather disgruntled about the intrusion. (Then in the future don't hold a woman hostage in your hotel room!)

As is obvious by this story, we as hotel employees do care about the health and well-being of our guests. When a situation arises, we do everything in our power to resolve the problem before we have to take the more serious measure of calling in the local police. Big brother is watching!

The Unwelcome Guest

Sometimes guests have trouble sleeping because they're just too hopped up on the day's events or they're chemically enhanced with prescribed medication or illegal substances like cocaine or meth. They might be feeling a little "Randy" and are looking for sex or more drugs; other times they're just bored and want someone to talk to.

One particular night a guest called down to the front desk and I caught the call. He said, "Aren't you the cute skinny girl with long curly brown hair at the front desk?"

I said, "Yes, that would be me since I'm the only one matching that description on duty at this time of night."

He said, "You're gorgeous! And I'd really like to talk to you."

I said, "Sir, unfortunately I'm under time deadlines and I really don't have the time to chat right now."

He kept asking personal questions and insisted that I stay on the phone with him. It made me feel very unsafe and uncomfortable, and I was doing my best to be professional and get him off the phone. Finally, after so many attempts trying to throw him off of his game, he said, "I'm coming down to the lobby; I'll be there in ten minutes!"

Now I'm really freaked out! I don't know what this guy looks like, and from the conversation I ascertained that he was looking for a sexual liaison, and I wasn't having any of it! So the next call I made was to my security officer to ask him to come to the lobby to dissuade this guest, and security was in the lobby almost immediately. Also, at that exact same time two uniformed LAPD officers strolled into my lobby just doing a nightly round. When I saw them, I called them over to the front desk and explained my situation and asked if anything could be done.

The officers were so wonderful and polite, and they said, "Yes, we will talk to him, and if necessary we will take him into custody." They quoted some sort of California penal code that covered just this type of situation, although I don't remember the exact code because it was so long ago.

True to his word, the guest showed up in my lobby and made a beeline towards me at the front desk! The LAPD officers saw him and quickly intercepted the guest before he even got within fifteen feet of the front desk! They took him aside and talked with him at length, and then they escorted the guest back up to his room where he stayed for the rest of the night with no further contact with me either by phone or in person.

I was never so happy to see L.A.'s finest in my lobby that night. This situation could have turned really bad really fast; and as it turned out, everything was fine. Props to both my security officer and the LAPD!

Crazy Nights

A four-star hotel with approximately 500 hundred rooms should be well staffed on a sold-out night with several functions going on. But sometimes the management just doesn't think things through, and we end up *dropping the ball* for our guests.

On this particular night we had not only a wedding party but also had a bar-mitzvah with each party hosting about 200 people. Many of those party attendees were staying the night at the hotel as well. Being in sold-out status, we were already "walking" guests to other hotels.

Two people arrived on travel vouchers but only one reservation was showing in the system. I began checking them in, and from across the front desk my co-worker reminded me that we were in sold-out status and that I should not check this guest in. The guest overhearing this became angry and agitated. He said to his companion "This is why we don't stay here anymore," and then said, "I'll go to another hotel." He then called his travel agent and handed his cell phone to me wherein the travel agent started reading me the riot act. I assured the agent that there were no problems and no cause for alarm and that their customer did have a room here.

A few minutes later a Royal Thai consulate arrived to check in. There were only four rooms reserved in the system and they needed seven rooms: six kings and one double. One was a VIP and he had a suite pre-blocked and we were sold out of doubles. This group stays with us on a regular basis. The suite was dirty and had razor blades and trash strewn all through it so we had to have a night houseman clean the room rather quickly. Which begs the question: why wasn't this room checked before our VIP arrived? We were out of roll-away beds so André had to take a taxi to a nearby hotel and borrow four roll-away beds in order to accommodate our guests. The Thai consulate had said that they had never had such poor service from us before.

And one guest who refused the "walk" suggested that we put a couple of roll-away beds into a banquet room and use that!

The guest in room 837 was threatening to call the police because there was a high-pitched buzzing sound in his room.

And Mr. Duek in room 524 was given a free meal in our restaurant due to housekeeping and he found cockroaches in his room!

The bar-mitzvah broke up very late, and children were running wild and screaming up and down the hallways of several floors causing a disturbance to many of our guests. There was no security on any floors with wild children, and the manager on duty asked the catering service to help them gather up the children and quiet them down because he wasn't going to get another noise complaint about the children.

The main ballroom ceiling started leaking and buckets were brought in to protect the carpet. The A/C went out in the hotel, and it was a balmy 90 degrees inside the hotel during the hottest part of the day, and as of 11 p.m. it still had not been fixed.

The wedding had started, and as the bride was walking down the aisle, children from the bar-mitzvah ran through their party. The manager on duty quickly grabbed the children and saved the day for that bride and groom.

A kitchen employee cut his finger and had to be rushed to the local ER for stitches.

The guest in room 536 received a call after midnight asking if he wanted his luggage delivered to him, but his luggage had already been delivered earlier in the day. He was very upset for being awoken.

Another guest had complained that his keys did not work so he had to go back down to the lobby, and when he did get into his room, it had not been serviced by housekeeping, and to add insult to injury his TV remote did not work and no one brought him a new one so he had to make yet another trip to the front desk.

For some reason there was broken glass in the tenth floor hallway strewn out over half of the floor. The houseman cleaned it up, only to find broken glass again throughout the hallway an hour later.

The carpet on the second floor was filthy and had to be cleaned.

And guests were angry that they had to wait hours for a simple roll-away bed to be delivered.

How could a four-star hotel drop the ball so badly? Management is so concerned with costs that they cut corners on customer service. That should never happen ever!

Fortunately, the Ramras wedding party and the winter bar-mitzvah went off without a hitch, and they were all very happy with our service.

It is nights like that that really made my job memorable.

Shake, Rattle, and Roll

Living in Los Angeles, hell, living anywhere in California, we all become acutely aware that we are living in earthquake territory. We have one of the largest earthquake fault lines in the continental United States right in our backyard. This is the story of one of our big quakes.

110

It was June 28, 1992, and it had been a rather uneventful night. Things were running well. We had made our 2:30 a.m. deadlines, and we were pretty much just sitting around in the back office shooting the breeze waiting for the hotel computers to come back on-line. I was working in a twelve-story hotel with close to 500 rooms. It was almost 5 a.m. and the morning check-out rush usually started at 6 a.m., so the lobby would be filling up in an hour. I was walking back out to the front desk when I suddenly felt that familiar rolling sensation under my feet. I instinctively knew that we were experiencing an earthquake! I didn't know if it was going to be a big one or just a little tumbler, so I wasn't taking any chances and I got into a doorway, as we are taught to do during a quake, and held on!

It was at that moment that the rolling sensation picked up momentum, and as my hands tightly clutched the doorway, I felt two or three really enormous jolts! I knew this was a big one and immediately started praying and hoping that this building wouldn't fall on me! Who knows how many hundreds of thousands of pounds of steel and concrete were over my head?

The quake lasted about 45 seconds to a minute, which is the norm for a quake, but it's enough time and energy to level a city!

The quake was over and the hotel was still standing! I thanked Jesus and began the process of contacting the engineer so that he could inspect the hotel for structural damage and we could determine if we had to start evacuating the guests. The elevators did their jobs by coming down to the lobby floor and holding. Then rather quickly the lobby began to fill up. Guests were coming down the stairwells and many people were in their night clothes. Pajamas, robes, negligees and even quite a few men just in their "tighty-whities." No one was really asking any of the staff what happened or what they should be doing. They were half asleep and just instinctively knew that they had to get to someplace safe, and the lobby just seemed to be that place.

The thing about the lobby was that there were several large chandeliers hanging from the ceiling. The chandeliers weighed about 1,000 pounds apiece, and hard pieces made out of a heavy resin were falling off the chandeliers and dropping onto the guests. The quake was over but the chandeliers were still swaying pretty wildly. It was just dumb luck that the hard resin pieces didn't actually hit anyone, because I'm sure a hit would have caused some damage to a skull!

About twenty minutes later we had our first aftershock. And the chandeliers that had settled down were back in motion. The crowd of guests let out a shriek, and then they started running around in circles trying to find something to hide under. I stood up and assured them that this was an aftershock, and that the engineers had assured me that the building was safe. I also asked them to stay out from under the chandeliers.

I ended up working overtime that morning for all the obvious reasons, and the whole time all I could think about was: *Is my house still standing? Are my kids okay?* I just wanted to get home and I couldn't get through to my house on the phone.

Later on in the morning things had settled down, there were no more aftershocks, and the guests were wildly excited about having experienced a real California earthquake and had survived to tell the story!

I finally got home at around 8:30 a.m., and all my kitchen cabinets were open and there was broken glass and canned goods all over. My kids were okay but justifiably freaked out. I grabbed a broom and started the cleanup.

Now that's what I call "A California wake-up call."

Chapter 7: Good Deeds and Favorites

Mister Can You Spare a Dime?

A guest Ms. Pentz called from Pennsylvania and said that her son was in the hospital and was being discharged but was unfamiliar with the area, and friends would be coming for him in the afternoon.

The staff at the hospital recommended our hotel for a place to stay, but our rate was a little too high for her budgetary allowances. I offered to call around to other hotels in the area. I did and no one was too much lower than us, and no one was willing to do a walk-in via the telephone.

After several dead-ends from other hotels in the area and hearing the obvious distress in this mother's voice for the concern of her son, I offered to match the lowest hotel rate in the area, which was $135.00 per night, and take the credit card information over the phone and wait for the fax copy in the morning. (A guest can use a credit card over the phone as long as they send a fax copy of both the front and back of the credit card and Driver's license and a signature to be kept on file by the accounting department).

The mother and son were extremely grateful for my assistance in this matter, and she did fax over the credit card information before the end of my shift at 6:30 a.m.

We're not all bad guys. Some of us actually go above and beyond the policies and procedures sometimes because we just have too. It is definitely on a case-by-case basis. Ultimately, we want our guest's business so we are going to do our best to accommodate everyone no matter what their situation may be.

Ingenuity

According to Mrs. Howard in room 824, the bed that her eleven-year-old son was sleeping on broke. The leg was bent and weak, so when the boy sat on the bed, the leg broke. This happened about midnight.

I asked her if she thought that the bed was unsafe, and she said, "Yes." I offered to move her to another room, but she declined saying that she had a lot of packing to do. I offered her a roll-away bed temporarily, and she also said "No" to that because it would take up too much room. She just requested that the hotel maintenance department please bring her another bed.

In the middle of the night we generally have no maintenance person on duty so bringing her another bed at that time was not an option. So I sent Security Officer Doug to assess the situation. Mrs. Howard was so upset that she started throwing the "lawsuit" word around. Doug managed to fix the problem by putting four one-inch-thick phone books under the corner of the bed to level it out. He then asked the eleven-year-old boy to jump on the bed to insure that it would be sturdy enough to get through the night. I did not offer a "comp" or a discount on her room. I left that up to management.

In a Hole

One night my parents had the opportunity to stay in the hotel. My co-worker checked them in, and then the bellman got

114

them settled into their room. My mom always stays up way past midnight, so I knew that I could go up to her room around 2 a.m. when I took a ten-minute break.

I called my mom's room first to make sure that they were still awake, and then I went up to their room. I knocked softly and then I let myself in with a spare key that I had grabbed from the front desk. As I stepped into the room, I could only see my step-father sitting on the bed, so I asked, "Where is my mom?"

He said, "She's right here," and I looked and still couldn't see her. As I walked up to the bed I finally saw my mother. Her side of the bed was about one foot lower than my step-dad's side. She was in a hole! It looked like the bed was swallowing her whole! I was mortified beyond all belief! I thought, *How does this happen in MY hotel?*

I got her up and out of bed, and then I called a bellman to assist me. We took off the sheets and flipped the mattress, and to our surprise one of the box springs had been turned upside down, which caused the mattress to sink into the frame! So we put everything back the right way, and my mom had a great night, but it's sure going to be one for the scrap book.

The Long Road Home

We had a guest named Mr. Bartolomeo who arrived on October 27 with his wife to attend a wedding and ended up extending his stay indeterminately when his wife became gravely ill and was admitted to the hospital on November 7. Mr. Bartolomeo approached the front desk and spoke to Desk Agent Lemie and advised her of his situation and asked if we could possibly offer him a lower rate because he would be here for at least one month's time, possibly longer, and he really could not afford to pay the $179.00 rate for that length of time. Lemie informed the guest that the rate could not be changed under any circumstances. He really loved the fact that we were right across the street from the hospital and that he could just walk there. Mr. Bartolomeo was distressed at having to leave us but said that he would be checking out immediately.

I looked at the guests account and I observed that Mr. Bartolomeo had already spent $2,000 in revenue here and was utilizing most of our services daily. I called Mr. Bartolomeo over to chat with him. I asked him what hotel he would be moving to. He said that our competitor was offering a rate of $120.00.

Seeing the revenue that he has already generated and being sensitive to his situation, without hesitation, I offered to match our competitor's rate of $120.00. Mr. Bartolomeo was absolutely ecstatic and thanked us for accommodating him in his time of need. Mr. Bartolomeo stayed with us for 30 days and generated $5,000 in revenue. Sadly his wife passed away. He had been a wonderful guest, and he had contact with almost every staff member at the front desk. In light of his loss, our hotel sent an arrangement of fresh flowers and a letter of condolence at the behest of the desk agents and night auditors.

Remember what I said about going "Above and beyond" the call of duty? While one desk agent shut this guest down, I was able to intercede and make the magic happen. Just because one employee won't work with a guest doesn't mean that the guest is "down for the count." I advise to keep inquiring and eventually there will be someone who will be willing and able to "Play ball."

Hijinks on the Night Audit

Someone downloaded a strange ICON onto the night auditor's terminal. It was a picture of actress Linda Blair as the Exorcist. We left a note concerning that item for the front desk manager to follow up. Very funny people, very funny!

Lost-and-Found Wallet

This is just an all-around feel-good story. A homeless man named Bernie walked into the lobby and turned in a wallet that he had found outside on the sidewalk. He thought that maybe it belonged to one of our guests. The wallet belongs to a Mr. G London. The only ID was a student travel card with a photo. There was also a:

- Bank of America ATM Visa check card
- Platinum MasterCard
- Chevron gas card in the name of R. Tafoya
- MCI calling card in the name of S. Serrano
- And other miscellaneous business cards and .05 cents. No cash was found.

I called the number on the MCI calling card and made contact with an R. Tafoya, who said that Mr. London was his son. He was very grateful for the call and gave me his son's address in Bakersfield, CA, to send his son' wallet.

Mr. Tafoya later called me back and said that he had left a voicemail on his son's cell phone for him to contact me (Christie) to retrieve his wallet. I let Mr. Tafoya know that the wallet will be with our security office in the lost-and-found bin.

It was very generous of Bernie to bring in Mr. London's wallet, and he wanted to know if there would be some sort of reward. I let Mr. Tafoya know, and he said his son would be more than happy to leave a little something for Bernie. I asked Bernie to check back with me in a few days to see if Mr. London had left something for him.

Bernie also let me know where he'd be: The Bank of America parking lot and also at the corner of Wiltshire and Hamilton Boulevards at the C-bar Theater.

Mr. London did arrive the next day to pick up his wallet, and as he promised, Mr. London left a $20.00 bill in an envelope at the front desk for Bernie.

Japanese Eggshells

When dealing in the business of international travelers, not only did we strive to give each and every person the ultimate customer service experience, but it was also important to be aware and cognizant of our guests' particular country and customs. It would be very easy to offend someone with a simple gesture or a simple accounting mistake, as this next story explains:

I received a phone call from Japan early one morning about 5 a.m. It was a former guest named Mr. Sato, who wanted to speak with the accounting department to lodge a complaint concerning his billing. I decided to help Mr. Sato because most billing errors are simple and easily resolved. When Mr. Sato checked in, his credit card was declined. He presented another card, and it also was declined, so Mr. Sato gave a $1,500 cash deposit.

Upon checkout, the desk agent informed the guest that he had a remaining credit balance on his account and then promptly refunded the guest in the amount of $526.95. Mr. Sato left the hotel very pleased with his entire experience, and he was looking forward to his return visit at the end of April.

Mr. Sato submitted an expense report to his company for reimbursement and was shocked to learn from his company that there had been an additional $578.75 charged to his company credit card after he left. Now Mr. Sato was being questioned as a possible fraud by his own company and was in a difficult position that could have jeopardized his livelihood. As this is a Japanese company, the repercussions for Mr. Sato would have been severe if this situation was not immediately resolved.

In Japan, honor and respect is of the utmost for all persons. *Your word is your bond* really means something in Japan. Men have committed the ultimate act of hari-kari due to loss of honor. I don't know if that type of behavior still goes on in Japan, but it goes to show just how serious Japanese people take their vows.

Understanding Mr. Sato's predicament, I wanted to provide him with some immediate answers. I apologized to Mr. Sato and assured him that there was no malicious intent with the actions of the hotel.

My research uncovered a gross error on the part of one of our desk agents. After Mr. Sato had checked out, some late charges were posted in the amount of $50.83. Somehow the desk agent thought that there was a credit balance of $526.95. So she created a "Pay out" slip. That confusion lead her to believe that there was now a balance of $578.75, so the desk agent charged the credit card on file in order to zero out the account. Boy, it was quite a piece of work! Additionally the desk agent failed to inform anyone of this gross error. If she had any auditor or anybody in the accounting department, the situation could have easily been handled. There was no phone number or address listed for Mr. Sato in Japan.

Mr. Sato's confidence in our hotel had justifiably been shaken, but he said that he still intended to return to our property because he really enjoyed his stay on the last trip. He stated, and for good reason, that he will in the future always deal with us on a cash-only basis.

Mr. Sato did not want to know my name because he had been intending to make a complaint about this matter. Because I was able to help him resolve his problem quickly and with a very good attitude, he did not want my name to be dishonored. Mr. Sato expressed his confidence in me to see this matter through to the proper personnel.

The Fight for Elian Gonzalez

One night around 2:30 a.m. my bellman and the valet parking attendant were standing in the lobby making small talk while the hotel was pretty quiet. There was a woman sitting on a couch nearby them. Somehow the topic of conversation got around to a six-year-old Cuban boy named Elian Gonzalez. He had made international news when his father and U.S. authorities had taken him by force from his relatives that were living in Miami, Florida. They had taken him at gun point and were wearing gas masks to deport him back to Cuba under his father's insistence that he be returned to Cuba. His mother had brought him over, but in the process of crossing the Atlantic Ocean, she unfortunately drowned. Immigration authorities placed him with relatives in Miami until they could figure things out. The bellman and the valet parking attendant we're talking a little loud and then they started laughing at the obscurity of how little Elian was taken at gun point.

It was at that point that the woman who was nearby on a couch could take no more of their, what she thought were disrespectful comments, and she couldn't stand idly by listening so she confronted the two men. As it turns out, the woman had only heard bits and pieces and made assumptions out of context. The two men were trying to explain themselves, but it only caused the woman to become more upset. Soon all three of them were yelling at each other. I saw what was happening, and I intervened on the hotel's authority. I asked what the problem was, and all three started talking at once. It was heated and it was escalating, so I said in a very commanding and authoritative voice "You two! Outside where you belong! I'll deal with you later!"

By now the woman was so frustrated and angry that she was actually crying. I deeply apologized for the behavior of my employees, and I asked her if there was anything I could do for her. She said that Elian was just a child that went through a horrific life event, first losing his mother and then being taken away from his family at gun point. She said that Elian must have been scared out of his mind and that no child should ever have to go through something like that. And for those two men to be laughing about it was downright tacky and crass. She said that they should have empathy for Elian; and if they are religious, then they should pray for Elian and his father.

I acknowledged how she was feeling and agreed with her that my two employees had been disrespectful of the situation. I also acknowledged that the workplace was not a place to be discussing these kinds of matters. She was relieved at my thoughtfulness and professionalism in handling the situation. She said that it could have gotten way out of hand if I hadn't intervened when I did. The woman had finally calmed down, and then we changed the topic to routine small talk. By the end of our conversation, I had her laughing and feeling good about the incident.

She wanted to tell my supervisor of how well I handled what could have been an ugly scenario. That made me feel good but I told her it was not necessary. I said "I'm just being a human being."

The rest of the night went off without a hitch. And I did speak with my bellman and valet parking attendant about what is and is not appropriate work talk. We dealt with people from all over the world with different values and ideas, and we never knew what simple things could offend or set someone off. I stressed that it is important to keep conversations to work-related issues only.

I always keep an open mind and the way I handle things is by agreeing to disagree, and you'd be surprised at how well that works.

Mrs. Landau

Sonia Landau was an older guest; if I had to guess she was in her mid to late 70's. She was short in stature with a tiny frame and locks of long shoulder-length hair and devastatingly deep blue eyes. She always traveled with a friend, her best four-legged friend, a Maltese dog named Bentley.

Now Bentley was always well-groomed and was an AKC-registered show-quality dog. He was also very well-mannered. Sonia lived in a very small town in Arizona, and she traveled a lot

121

to both New York City and Los Angeles for work. She never did elude to exactly what it was that she did for a living except to say that it was very important work. She needed plenty of rest and a quiet space to work in. She always requested and revived room number 1030, a handicapped accessible room on the eighth floor. She liked the room because it was much more spacious than ordinary rooms, due to the fact that it could accommodate a wheelchair, and the other fact that most disabled persons choose not to smoke. My particular hotel had a generous pet policy, meaning that we accepted pets during our guests stay at no additional charge to our guests. Sonia loved to come down to the lobby and strike up conversations with everyone from the front desk staff to the concierge and bellmen, and her conversations were always interesting.

There was a time when my own dog, a Chihuahua named Tootsie, fell ill. She had some sort of heart problem, so in order to keep a close eye on her and give her medications, I started bringing her to work with me. One of those times, Sonia was in the house, so it was really neat to introduce Tootsie to Bentley. Tootsie was a female. Bentley, of course, was male; and the two dogs made fast friends. Sonia and I would walk the two dogs around the hotel in the middle of the night to take them on bathroom breaks. The two dogs looked forward to seeing each other at night and it was quite a sight to see!

Everyone got used to Sonia and Bentley showing up every month, and we always made sure to reserve her favorite room and stock up on treats for Bentley. She was in our hotel every month for over a year, but then she stopped coming. We never did find out why. We could only assume that either she had retired or she had passed away, and we wondered whatever became of our favorite four-legged guest Bentley. He was always so dashing and debonair—total show quality!

A Dillar, a Dollar, a 10 o'clock Scholar

Once in a while a hotel employee has to go above and beyond the call of duty. Those times are far and few between but always memorable.

This story is about a guest who left her pocketbook in the lobby one morning while she was waiting for her car to be brought up. Bear in mind that the LAX Airport was 35 miles away through heavy traffic. My co-worker and I spotted the pocketbook and immediately put a plan into motion. The outcome was positive. The following is the letter of praise that we received from the guest:

Dear Mr. Martin (our general manager at the time),

I've just returned from my fourth stay at your hotel. Twice a year I come with a contingent of my staff from Emerson College to conduct alumni meetings and events throughout Los Angeles. We first discovered your hotel a few years ago, and everyone has loved the ambiance at your hotel so much that we simply book with you each time we come out. However, like so many of your visitors, we have never taken the time to congratulate you and your staff on the wonderful way that the hotel is run.

This time is different for a very good reason. We left the hotel at 5 a.m. on this Tuesday. After waiting for everyone to convene in the lobby, I managed, as we left, to leave my pocketbook on a lobby chair (so concerned with getting all my staff's luggage into our rental car etc.). I didn't discover this until I got to the Avis car rental, had already given back the car, and went to board the shuttle bus. You can imagine my hysteria, especially since in these days of airport security, there was no way I could catch my flight home without my identification, etc.

I called the hotel in a panic. They had already discovered the bag and had tried to figure out ways to contact me. They immediately took over and made a plan to get my bag out to me at the airport, stayed with me on the phone so that they could give me the specifics on the cab company and cab number, arranged a specific place for him to meet me, etc. I have to tell you that Jennifer and Christie could not have been more wonderful. They not only acted with astonishing efficiency but they kept me calm with their ability to handle the situation. Everything was so efficient that I made my flight with time to spare.

I'm extremely grateful as you can imagine. I hope you appreciate their good work as well for I know that the overnight staff are often unsung heroes. If I liked your hotel before, I love it now. Thank you and all your staff for always making our visits so pleasant, and special thanks to Christie and Jennifer for a job well done.

Best Wishes,
J.M.B., Vice President, International Advancement

Not everyone will go out of their way to make the right thing happen in this kind of a scenario. Most likely what would have happened if Jennifer and I had not intervened on this guest's behalf is that the pocketbook would have been turned over to security and would have been locked up in a secure cabinet or in a secure storage room with absolutely no attempts being made to locate the owner and figure out how to get it to her.

But Jennifer and I, being cognizant and highly aware of what grief and hassle this woman would have gone through not knowing what had become of her pocketbook, and then going through the hassle of canceling all her credit cards and reapplying for her identification and losing sentimental family photos that she had been keeping in her pocketbook. Well, that was just all bad, and we really felt for her so we went out of our way to make it right.

124

I wish everyone could have that attitude. Jennifer and I also came across more than our fair share of lost cell phones, too. In those cases, we would just go through the "recent calls" list or find their "favorites" list and call the last person that the guest had called and said something to the effect of: "This is the hotel and we found this cell phone in the lobby. If you know who this belongs to can you please contact them and let them know that their phone will be kept in our security office until they can come to retrieve it." We had around a 99% success rate with that method and saved a lot of people some heartaches.

Cash Flow

Many hotels have a check-cashing policy for the convenience of their guests. It eliminates the need for a guest to have to find their particular bank in and around the area and hope that it's open and/or finding an ever-elusive ATM machine that charges small fees for dispensing cash from their accounts. My particular hotel had a $150-a-day personal check-cashing limit with a cap of $500 per stay. For the purposes of this story I will call this particular guest, guest X.

Now I had checked guest X in on my shift at around 11:30 p.m. that night, and he was slated to stay with us for seven days. The next morning as I was about to clock out and head home at 7:30 a.m., guest X showed up at the front desk and asked to cash $150 personal check. I said, "No problem," and I processed his check and gave him his cash. The very next morning guest X again appeared at the front desk at close to 7:30 a.m. and again wanted to cash a $150 personal check. This time I was actually a little suspicious of guest "X" because he had just cashed $150 check the day before. I made some small talk trying to figure out what was really going on, but I went ahead and cashed his check. The third day, guest "X" was again at the front desk at 7:30 a.m.

wanting to cash a $150 check. This time, however, I ran the check and guest X's story and my concerns past my supervisor.

My supervisor said, "Go ahead and cash his check." However, I asked my supervisor to put his own initials on the back of the check to show that he had in fact personally authorized this check. I was thinking about covering my own ass in case it turned out badly.

Sure enough, day four rolled around, and here was guest X at 7:30 a.m. again. And again cashing a $150 check. Again, I had my supervisor put his initials on the check.

Every day of his seven-day stay, guest X had cashed a personal check far exceeding the $500 limit imposed by the hotel, with the approval of my direct supervisor. I had a bad feeling about this, and each day I had adamantly protested cashing guest X's checks. Day seven and guest X checked out with his final $150 check cashed.

Ten days after guest X checked out his, checks started hitting our bank and they started bouncing! Every check that guest X had written bounced! Now, I had fought tooth-and-nail with my supervisor Fred every time guest X had wanted to cash a check because I knew they were going to bounce. I mean this this guy had "red flags" going off everywhere. But Fred just wanted to provide the best possible customer service, regardless of the situation. And what's more, the human resources department called me into a meeting with Fred to talk about guest X's transactions. HR and upper management basically told me that I was being held personally liable for reimbursing the hotel for every one of those bounced checks because I was the one who had ultimately cashed them and had disregarded the check-cashing limit policy. They even told me that I would have to go to the address listed on the front of the check and personally collect the $1,000 from guest X, and I'd have to do it on my own time; and if I did not, then the $1,000 would be coming out of my paycheck! I couldn't believe what I was hearing!

I said, "Fred personally authorized those checks against my protests. So if anyone should be held liable it should be Fred!"

I further stated that California State Labor Law says that cashiers are NOT to be held personally liable for fraudulent cash transactions. And I wasn't about to go down without a fight! I got up from the meeting and said, "I quit! See you in court!"

I did quit that day, and the hotel never contacted me again with regards to guest X and his woeful money problems.

What are people going to do?
Fire me? I've been fired before.
Not book me? I've been out of work before.
I don't care.

~ Joan Rivers

The key is to set realistic customer expectations, and then not to just meet them, but to exceed them—preferably in unexpected and helpful ways.

~ Sir Richard Branson

Chapter 8: More Odds and Less Ends

Minibar Pirates!

A guest under the name of Mr. Jones had an internet reservation through Travelscape.com. Mr. Jones had three rooms: 924, 926, and 928. No credit card was taken at the time of his check-in for incidentals, yet somehow Mr. Jones was able to secure a minibar key.

They had checked out rather early in the morning before the minibar attendant could check the room, and they did not indicate that they had taken anything out of the minibars. No desk agent asked about incidentals because no deposit was taken at check-in, and it was assumed that no incidental charges had been incurred. When the attendant did check the room, he found that all three rooms had their minibars cleaned out to the tune of $600.00!

I went back to the reservation's computer and looked up the billing information and found a Travelscape MasterCard. I then charged that credit card per the internet agreement for the minibar charges, even though I expected there may be some sort of backlash from Travelscape.

A hotel will use every resource available to recoup incidental charges, so honesty is the best policy for guests when checking out early. When guests honestly do not take anything from the minibar or don't watch a pay-per-view movie, it is very important that they let the front desk know at check-out so the bill can be adjusted accordingly.

Wakey, Wakey, Wakey

What happens in a four-star hotel when someone misses a wake-up call?

The guests in room 740 missed their wake-up call this morning at 4:45 a.m., and as per hotel procedure we dispatched a bellman to knock on the door. Still no answer. Then we authorized the security officer to gain entrance to the room for a health and welfare check. The male and female occupants appeared to be alive and breathing normally but seemed to be under the influence of something that had most likely put them into a deep sleep from which they could not awaken when the security officer attempted to wake them. Since they appeared to be in no mortal danger, the security officer closed and locked the door. We needed to send someone up to the room every hour or so until they woke up.

As I stated in an earlier story, large hotels average between two and four dead bodies a month. So we take a rather proactive stance in dealing with missed wake-up calls and rooms that still have their "Do not disturb" signs up well after check-out time at 11 a.m. If there is no answer, there will be someone checking the room.

Aren't We Nice?

Dear Sir or Madame,

Here are some of the packages that are available to our guests:

1. Box of chocolates
2. Large fruit basket
3. Wine and cheese
4. Chocolate strawberries
5. Pineau des Charentes and nuts

Flowers can also be arranged through the hotel's concierge. I hope this will help you and your wife have a great Valentine's Day!

Regards,
Christie S – Night Auditor

Courteous treatment will make a customer a walking advertisement.
~ James Cash Penney

Jet Lagged

On a cold March morning, I received two phone calls from outside of the hotel asking for a guest who was neither listed in the "Arrivals" nor the "Canceled" reservations list. I did, however, take the message for a guest named Shani.

The guest named Shani did arrive sometime later that evening, but we did not have a reservation for her in the system. She was traveling under a group travel itinerary from Qantas Airlines, also known as Qantas Holiday, under which her room and tax were prepaid by Qantas Airlines. My co-auditor, Jennifer, got on the line to Qantas to try and get the whole mix up straightened out. However, she was put on hold and Qantas never picked up the line. The guest Shani was becoming more and more agitated as Jennifer and I tried our best to accommodate her. Meanwhile, I decided to check her into a room at the Qantas rate, and I asked her for a credit card or a cash deposit for any incidental charges. The card that she gave me declined authorization for $50, and this was the minimum "hold" that we would place on a credit card. She asked for her room key and then she went on her way.

During the initial check-in, the guest was obviously agitated, and she continued to complain about all the flight delays she had encountered throughout her day. She also vocalized her extreme dislike of Qantas Airlines, saying, "Qantas has a monopoly on Australia. You can't take any other airlines out of Australia unless you are willing to pay an additional $3,000!" She continued, "The service is lousy, the flights are bad, and the food is unpalatable."

Ms. Shani also complained about the service here at the hotel. She said, "I've stayed here every March and every September for the last six years and never once has anyone said to me, 'Welcome back.' What kind of service is that?" I apologized for the oversight and told her that I hoped that we can do something to improve our service.

When Ms. Shani arrived at her room, she wanted to place a call to Australia but found that her phone was blocked. She called down and spoke to Jennifer who again repeated the policy on incidental charges. She asked for someone to come to her room to take a deposit. I sent the night bellman, Francis, and the guest handed Francis a $50 bill, but she demanded that he write her a receipt on the spot. Francis explained to the guest that he did not have the ability to write her a receipt but that he would give the deposit to the front desk and return with a receipt for her. I heard the guest yelling at Francis, "Get out of my room right now!"

Moments later, Ms. Shani appeared at the front desk and proceeded to throw a $50 bill at me and said that this was terrible service, and she asked to speak to a manager immediately! Ms. Shani said that this incident was going to cost the hotel much more than the $50 deposit.

I explained that there was no manager on duty at this late hour, so she asked and expected to speak to a manager in the morning. She said that she hopes that there will be a lot of people around when she does because she's going to get really loud!

The woman was visibly upset at a lot of things that had gone wrong during her entire day and was jet lagged from an 18-hour flight. It seemed that after a good night's rest she felt better and nothing more seriously came out of this incident.

We got a lot of the brunt of travelers' anger and frustrations and had to remind ourselves that it was not our fault when guests had a lousy day. And sometimes we dropped the ball by failing to acknowledge a repeat guest with a simple greeting, and obviously that should not ever happen in a four-star hotel—or any hotel for that matter. Simple guest service was paramount to our hotel's reputation, and management just had to be mindful of delicate or volatile situations and do whatever was necessary to make said guests feel welcome at our hotel.

The Internet Revolution

The internet is very much here to stay. People now keep all their important as well as personal information in the "Cloud," which is someplace out in time and space. We can do anything and everything through the internet. We can watch our homes remotely as well as turn on and off our lights and appliances. We can Skype with our personal physician, our co-workers, and our family. We have instant access to nearly every book, TV show, and data base in the world. It takes all the blood, sweat, and tears out of doing research the old-fashioned way.

This story happened back in the day when internet access was still of the "dial up" version. Hotels saw the money-making potential of the internet and began offering internet access in every room—for a fee, naturally. They touted internet access, but when a guest arrived in their rooms, there were absolutely no instructions posted anywhere in the room, or in the entire hotel for that matter, of how to access the internet from the guest rooms. All that was there was what was called a "data port" for guests to plug their devises into the wall.

133

Mr. Pachulski stayed as our guest for five days and generated $1,400 in revenue during his stay. And while he loved our hotel, his problem was that he couldn't access the internet, and that was one of the main reasons that he chose to stay at our hotel. He called several different hotel departments asking for instructions on how to access the internet and was given several different answers. It seemed no employee of the hotel knew exactly how to access the internet. Most hotels are like office buildings in regards to making telephone calls where guests have to dial 9 to get an outside line.

The process was cumbersome to get on the internet at our hotel. First, the guest had to dial *9, get an outside line, then disable the call-waiting feature by dialing 7-0. At that point, a guest could access the internet by dialing into one of their databases. There was much confusion concerning the whole process; this greatly frustrated guests and ultimately got them angry and impatient.

Mr. Pachulski wound up having to take a cab ride up to the local Kinko's to access his email and internet. When he checked out, he said that he would not be returning to our hotel; and furthermore, he wanted a letter of apology sent to him from our hotel management. He was a true gentleman in dealing with this issue, and so I recommended that management make every effort to accommodate Mr. Pachulski in hopes that he would want to make a return visit.

Nowadays, there is very seldom dial-up service. Are EarthLink and AOL still around? I'd have to check with my computer-savvy friends on that one. Now we can wirelessly access the internet from our smartphones, tablets, or laptops. Usually, all we need is a password. I myself stayed in a hotel recently that had to have a password for internet access, and no one at the hotel knew what the password was! Great customer service!

Places like Target and Walmart now have Wi-Fi, and they don't require a password. Makes life 100% simpler. I can only hope that hotels pick up on this little tidbit of information and implement it into their systems, for those who haven't already.

Cry Baby Cry

People always expect to get what they ask for. And really why shouldn't they get precisely what they ask for? They are paying good, hard-earned cash for a service that they want and that was advertised as available. But often times, that's not the case when a guest arrives at a hotel.

Rooms at a hotel are given out on a first-come first-serve basis. Things like two beds versus one bed in the room, smoking or non-smoking, handicap access, bottom floor versus a higher floor, poolside, etc. The list goes on forever. The hotel staff makes every conceivable effort to get guests what they asked for, but on nights with higher occupancy, such as Friday and Saturday nights, they can't always guarantee that what any particular guest asked for will be available. Sometimes there is trouble.

Mr. Dubois was checking into the hotel. He'd had a long day and a few things had gone wrong. He missed a connecting flight because his flight was overbooked and he couldn't board, which in turn made the airline lose his luggage because it had made the flight and he didn't. He had a long day of meetings planned for the next morning, and he just wanted to get to his hotel and get a good night's rest.

When Mr. Dubois arrived and began the check-in process, he had reserved a room with two double beds. However, it was a Friday night and the hotel was in sold-out status. We had just enough rooms to cover our incoming reservations for the evening, and what was left was very slim pickings. I informed Mr. Dubois that there weren't any rooms with two double beds available, but we did have a room that had a king bed and was considered to be an upgrade from the rate that he was paying; and that because of his inconvenience, we wouldn't be charging him any extra fees.

Mr. Dubois got very upset and made his argument about the reservation to which I just went into the hotel policy spiel. I offered to let Mr. Dubois look at the room before he committed to actually check in, and he accepted my offer. Jennifer, my relief night auditor, took him up to the room. He wasted a lot of precious time arguing the small points of the room. As I've stated before, night auditors are on a very strict time schedule, so we can't stand around all night and argue with a guest. We've got to be highly professional, pleasant, and diplomatic in curtailing a conversation with a guest.

Nothing we offered Mr. Dubois was satisfactory to him. Finally I told Mr. Dubois that he could take what we have available or we could find him a comparable room at another hotel. That, of course, would be on our dime. He did not want to leave so he checked in.

I left a note with the morning supervisor to be sure and change Mr. Dubois to a double bedded room as soon as one was available. Mr. Dubois also asked that I thoroughly advise my supervisor about the situation and wanted to speak directly to my supervisor and did not want to have to repeat himself.

Just because a guest throws a tantrum or cause a scene doesn't mean that they will get what they want right at that moment. We are a business and we are willing to work with a guest, but the guest has to be flexible and hopefully understanding of our circumstances.

The Complaint Department

Every job in America has had their fair share of problems. Customers complain and employees complain and it seems as if nothing ever gets resolved. This is a list of complaints that the hotel employees had made over the course of a year.

1. The reservation department starts their shift at 7 a.m. and quite frequently they aren't ready to start taking reservations until 7:15 a.m., and it seems that the reservations department gets a lot of "sick calls," this causing stress and inconvenience to the front desk, which is already overwhelmed by check-outs in the early morning hours. I would highly recommend cross-training for every front desk agent in the reservations department. I find that in my attempt to make a reservation for a guest, I am unfamiliar with rates and codes. So I always quote rack rate of $289.00.

2. There has been an increase in guest complaints primarily in "wait time" and "undercooked" food from the restaurant. Undercooking food to me is simply a matter of self-opinion. Everyone has a different view or idea on how something should be prepared. You can't please some of the people all the time. So I think that is a moot issue. The "wait time" for food, however, is something that can be resolved. We could hire more waiters or just have the bus boys help out during peak hours at the restaurant. I am open to suggestions here.

3. The soft-drink machine is constantly breaking down and serves only warm soda, even if you put it into an ice-filled glass. The hot-cocoa machine: the inner circular container (that holds the dry cocoa mixture) has large unsightly holes in it that looks as if somehow the plastic was melted. This can allow bugs to get into the dry cocoa mixture. The metal lid that covers the cocoa machine is also broken and has fallen off and nearly hit me several times.

4. The locks on all the liquor cabinets and wine cabinets at the bar don't work at all. They are just there for looks, and anyone can open the cabinets and walk off with any liquor they chose. Case in point: two gentlemen made off with a

couple of bottles of Cristal champagne last week. I've reported this as well as have the bartenders, and it's been like that for more than a year. What's up with that?

5. The dishwasher needs to pay more careful attention to his duties because quite often when I am in the kitchen, room service, or the employee cafeteria, I have found food particles on clean dishes and glasses! Yuck!

6. On the third floor there is an exhaust fan for the air conditioning and ventilation system. The fan is connected to a slotted vent on the exterior of the building. One of the slots on the vent broke loose and was banging on the vent creating a low noise that can specifically be heard in the guest rooms at night when there is little activity going on in the hotel. I even spent the night and stayed in room 303, and I could hear the vent flapping rhythmically all night long from about 2 a.m. to 6 a.m. Although it didn't bother me, I can understand how annoying it could be to other guests! I reported the noise weeks before my stay, and I continued to report it for three weeks after. I had to move many guests during the night, specifically because of the noise from the fan. WHY? Why did it take six weeks to fix that? It's unbelievable and distressing because it was so unnecessary!!

7. A drain stopper in the women's second-floor restroom (the one adjacent to the grand staircase) was reported by me as stuck in the down position and wasn't allowing the water to drain out of the wash basin. I personally reported this to three different members of the engineering department on three different occasions. The drain stopper went un-repaired for four months! Disgraceful!

8. Again the same restroom, the first stall door lock is in bad shape. I've reported it three times in two months. Again nothing has been done about it!

9. The carpet in the PBX department needs to be re-stretched. Bubbles are forming in the center and could pose a safety threat. Also I've been seeing spiders and small weevils in the PBX. How about getting the bug man to spray back there on the night audit when we can let it air out safely?

10. Some guests are particularly fussy about the way their rooms are made up, and they often have simple requests. Quite often the first thing housekeeping asks me is, "How much are they paying?" Now this to me sounds absolutely absurd!! Why does it matter what the guest is paying? The service should be the same no matter what the guest is paying. Here is just a small list of some of the requests that I get on a regular basis:
    1. Extra hand towels
    2. Extra soap/lotion
    3. Extra pillows/foam pillows (non-allergenic)
    4. Extra blankets
    5. Bottled water
    6. Toothbrush/toothpaste
    7. Correctly fitting sheets/pillow cases
    8. Bed made too tight
    9. No service today
    10. Air freshener
    These are routine items that should NEVER BE QUESTIONED by housekeeping when a guest requests it. Too often I get excuses from housekeeping on why it can't be done.

11. Guests frequently comment on the fact that the toilet paper is very rough for a four-star hotel. Believe me, guests do comment!

12. On a night with high occupancy expected, housekeeping should not go home early, and we should NEVER have VACANT DIRTY rooms in the system after 11 p.m.

13. The guest in room 1030 some months ago reported a broken sink leg in her room. She has since returned on three separate occasions and found the same sink leg still broken. When housekeeping cleans rooms, they should also be reporting things like that to engineering. (Come on housekeeping; what's going on?)

14. Many of the housekeepers are not proficient in simple English speaking. I find myself having to get someone to translate a guest's request too often, which slows the guest's service. (How about E.S.L. Classes?)

The requests are varied and often times not addressed by the hotel management for whatever reasons they have for not doing it. But a four-star hotel should be addressing these issues immediately, not months down the road. And with guests paying upwards of $300.00 a night, none of these complaints should be an issue.

Let's Make a Deal

Large hotels usually have contracts with tourist travel groups and international airlines. We get tour buses and airline crews on a daily basis, and that's really the hotels "bread and butter." It's a lot of bodies. We can have upwards of five to ten flight crews with five or more airline employees, depending on the size of the aircraft and from where they were flying. And that could be up to 50 rooms a night at around $75 to $100 a pop. The tourist buses have a lot more people and could be 50 to 60 people per bus with an average of three to five buses a day. That's close to 250 people at $75 to $100 a pop. So we're talking easily 300 rooms a night for a total ranging from $22,000 to $30,000 revenue every night; that's more or less depending on the specific contracted rates with each company. And of course those guests are spending additional dollars in our gift shops, restaurants, and optional local sightseeing tour packages that the hotel offers.

One thing many of those particular guests (since they're international travelers) do is buy items in bulk for steeply discounted prices in the U.S. and take them back to their countries of origin and sell them at a profit—because they are either not available, are too costly or are just not of high enough quality from manufacturers and importers in their own countries.

This is especially true of countries like Australia, Mexico, and the Philippines. I've been out on the town shopping with crews from Mexicana Airlines when they hit the garment district in downtown Los Angeles where they look for and buy lingerie and women's bathing suits in bulk. I've seen the Philippines Airline crews come through the lobby with four to eight full-sized new car tires, cases of disposable baby diapers, and cases of American breakfast cereal.

There really is no end to what they'll buy and take back home. Some have said it is for profit, and others are just trying to provide savings and convenience for their families who are in need.

Therefore, despite what people say about the quality of foreign products being imported from other countries, it often is better being "Made in America."

I Get By with a Little Help from My Friends

Summer season at a four-star hotel can get pretty busy with corporate symposiums, wedding receptions, family reunions, bar mitzvahs, and everything thing in between going on in our banquet rooms at one time or another. The parties can go on into the wee hours of the morning, and we can expect to be calling cabs for people that have had just one too many so that they get home in one piece. Quite often they either already have a room reserved or they stumble out of the party and stagger up to the desk and check in without a reservation, which is ultimately the right decision.

On this particular night there was a birthday party for the lead singer in a popular local band, and one of the attendees was a girl who had just been fired from the hotel not a week before. As a matter of fact, the entire party plan was all her idea and was all planned out and set up months before she was fired, so it would have been a major inconvenience to change venues at the last minute, so the party plans moved forward. The party went well into the night, and it finally started to fizzle out about 2 a.m. However, I had noticed my former coworker and really good friend having an exceptionally difficult time navigating the lobby floor. She was fumbling around for her keys, and as a friend I just had to intervene on her behalf. Now mind you, this wasn't the first time that I had seen her inebriated beyond all capacity. She was definitely a hard-core party animal. But I also knew that she was a blackout drinker who would have absolutely no recollection of any of the events from the night before, so putting her in a cab and sending her home was not a viable option, as far as I was concerned.

The hotels have provisions in place if an employee or one of their family members wants to stay there on a rock-bottom discounted rate for both convenience for our out-of-town relatives that have popped in unexpectedly, and for the opportunity for the employee to have the real-life experience of being a guest at such a nice establishment. It's just good business, good PR all the way around.

However, this girl was now a former employee and was certainly not my blood relative. Therein lied my dilemma. I couldn't in good conscience put her in a cab and send her home, and I obviously couldn't take her home myself, and it was 2 a.m., so who was I going to call to come and get her?

I had to take a gamble. The first mistake I made was that I took out my own credit card and checked her into a room at my employee rate. I indeed felt total relief when I got her upstairs and put her to bed without anything going terribly wrong. The second mistake that I made was not telling anyone from the hotel management what I had done and why I had done it.

During the day shift the front desk agents do what we call a "bucket check;" that is we have a file box where we place all the registration cards behind tabs that have each individual room number on them. Periodically throughout the day, desk agents go through the files and pull out any old registration cards from people that have long since checked out and place them in a more permanent file box in the basement. One of the things we're checking for is to ensure that the correct person is in the correct room and that all their information, e.g. address and credit card, is in the system. Because if we're too busy we just set the registration cards aside and catch up later when it dies down a bit.

At any rate, one of the girls noticed my name and my credit card on a registration card during the "bucket check." She also noticed that the alternate name on the room was a former employee. Yes. I had a lot of explaining to do.

Management called me in for a meeting that afternoon, and although they were sensitive to the situation and understood why I did what I did and that my heart was certainly in the right place, I had in fact violated several company policies in doing so. At that point they chose to terminate my employment and wished me well in my future endeavors.

I was glad that I did what I did and I wouldn't hesitate to do it again in order to save the life of a friend or possibly some random stranger's life by preventing a deadly car accident or worse. After all, I can get a job anywhere but I can't replace a human being.

Post Script

So there you have it—some of the things that happen on the night shift at a four-star hotel or any hotel that has banquet rooms, a cocktail bar, and restaurants. The auditors are busy trying to do the end-of-day calculations, postings, and rebates because everything has to be finished no later than 2:30 a.m. so that the computer can be taken off-line to run the room and tax and other reports.

One hotel that I was at switched operating systems from an old outdated version called H.I.S. and put in a new system called FIDELIO. Everything had to be manually input into the new system. This included all the guest checks that we refer to as "folios," and for months after we had numerous computer problems posting to the new system because everyone was still learning the system including the night auditors. After long nights on the phone with technical support and several visits from an actual technician, we finally got all the bugs worked out and the audit ran smoothly.

Dealing with everything else that cropped up concerning guest problems and guest requests just made life more difficult for the auditors. Just as J. Brodeur, the woman from Emerson College explained it, "The night auditors are truly the unsung heroes of the hotel." Not every front desk agent will give you what you're asking for and in that case just wait for the night audit crew to show up at 11 p.m. Because we are much more sensitive to your needs and we have the authority to make the decisions that will ultimately help you have a really great stay at our hotel. Just don't abuse the privilege.

"Peace out" and we will see you next time around.

I AM A FRONT DESK CLERK
AUTHOR UNKNOWN

A Little Sarcasm for Fun

I have an advanced degree in accounting, public relations, marketing, business, computer science, civil engineering, and Swahili.

Of course I have the reservation that you booked six years ago, even though you don't have a confirmation number and you think it was under a last name that begins with the letter "X".

It's not a problem for me to give you seven connecting, non-smoking, poolside suites with two king beds in each and four roll-away beds. And YES, I can install a wet bar. I know it's my fault that we do not have a helicopter landing pad.

I am a front desk clerk. I am expected to speak all languages. It is obvious to me that when you booked your reservation for Friday that you really meant Saturday. My company has entrusted me with financial information and decisions, and yet I can't tell you why your bill for March 1989 contained a $.25 phone call, because obviously you NEVER pay for phone calls.

I understand that McGillicuddy's Widget Manufacturing is a vast empire that will make or break our hotel. YES, I am lying when I say we have no more rooms available. It is not a problem for me to quickly construct several more guest rooms. This time I will not forget the helicopter landing pad.

I am a front desk clerk. I am quite capable of checking three people in, two people out, taking five reservations, answering fifteen incoming calls, and plunging the toilet in room 221 all at the same time.

I always know where to find the best restaurant— vegetarian/kosher/Moroccan BBQ. I know exactly what to see and do in the city in fifteen minutes without spending any money.

I take personal blame for the airline food, traffic jams, rental car flat tires, the location of our hotel, and the national economy.

I realize you meant to book your reservations here. People often confuse us with the Galaxy Delight Motel of Antarctica. Of course I can "fit you in;" and YES, you may have the special one-dollar corporate rate because you are affiliated with the Hoboken Accounting and Bagel Club.

I am expected to smile, empathize, sympathize, console, cajole, up sell, down sell (and know when to do which), perform, sing, dance, and fix the printer.

I am a front desk clerk. I do all things and still try to look busy when management is around.

Appendix: Advice for the Readers

When paying with a credit card, your ID must match the name on the card.

When paying cash without a credit card, expect to pay a rather large but totally refundable cash deposit. Give yourself a little extra time at checkout for the desk clerks to ensure that all your charges are correct.

If a hotel has in-room minibars, you will not be granted access to said minibar unless you either leave a credit card or an at least a $600-cash deposit at check-in.

A hotel will use every resource available to recoup incidental charges, so honesty is the best policy when checking out early. If you honestly did not take anything from the minibar or you didn't watch that pay-per-view movie, let the staff know upon checkout so your bill can be adjusted.

Don't try to intimidate the staff into getting what you want by playing the cards: "Do you know who I am?" Or "I can make one phone call?" These tactics almost never work. We will give you allowances within reason. Just be nice to the desk clerk.

Be polite upon registering for a room. Being rude to a front desk agent can get you put into the worst rooms in the hotel such as the noisiest, the most inaccessible, the most haunted! Really!

You can be sure that if you have an unusual or humorous name, every employee will probably be made aware of it. Sorry, there is no harm intended; it's just human nature.

Feel free to ask about special amenities such as fresh flowers, chocolates, fruit baskets, and if the hotel allows pets, something special for Fido.

Hotel management frowns on guests giving extra special employees gifts and or tips. So if one employee stood out to you and really made your stay special and you want to reward him or her, please do it on the sly or write a wonderful letter to their manager or leave a Comment Card.

Hotels have a lot of cash on hand during the day shift when the front desk is fully staffed. There's more than enough to cash a check or to get an advance on your credit card without incurring ATM fees if the hotel you're staying at offers those amenities. Check with the front desk when you check in; you just may save yourself some fees.

Special rooms such as smoking versus nonsmoking, handicap accessible, one bed versus two beds, ground floor or top floor, etc. are given on a first-come first-serve basis! Period. Just because you have a reservation doesn't guarantee your specific room, especially on nights with high occupancy. Calling ahead may help, so you may give it a try but don't be disappointed if it doesn't work.

Catastrophic failure: in cases where the mainframe goes down, your bills might not be ready at check out. In this case be sure that your correct address and/or correct fax number is noted on your registration card. The hotel will mail or fax your complete bill when the mainframe comes back on line. No amount of yelling, ranting, or threatening will get your bill any sooner.

Hotel handymen are more commonly known as engineers and are only on staff from 8 a.m. to 11 p.m. After that, if you are experiencing some kind of electrical or plumbing problem, the only recourse is to move you to another room until the problem can be dealt with in the morning.

Many large hotels have employees who speak more than one language. If you need a translator, have the reservationist make a note of it so that they can be prepared when you check in.

Some situations find you needing but unable to afford a four-star hotel for whatever reasons. An example would be if you need to stay near a hospital but could only afford a 1-Star hotel twenty miles away. On those occasions a hotel can and sometimes will agree to "Match" the rate at that 1-Star hotel for one to three nights. Just call directly and ask.

Wake up calls: if you miss your wake-up call, meaning if you fail to answer your phone call, an alert is set off at the hotel's main switchboard. The hotel will then dispatch bell staff, housekeeping, or a security guard to knock on your door to do a welfare check. If there is still no answer, then they will enter your room to investigate and make sure that you're okay.

A separate company contracted by the hotel usually hires the valet parking staff, so if you have a problem, it's best to talk to the valet manager directly.

Hotels will pay to have your personal items repaired or replaced if it has been proven that the damage was caused by the hotel staff.

There are times when a hotel can lock a person out of their room and not allow them back in. The reasons are varied and it's done at the sole discretion of hotel management. Be aware.

If the hotel has a concierge, take advantage of him or her. This staff member can set up practically anything your heart desires, from sightseeing tours, to shows, dinner reservations, and so on. You can ask for anything within reason, and he or she will be happy to help you. Yes, guests frequently ask for deliveries of street drugs like marijuana, cocaine, etc. and even ask for hook-ups with prostitutes. Most staff won't ever admit to it, but in some cities, they have secured those requests for guests.

When you get to your hotel, you just want to relax, unwind, and have a decent night's sleep without being woken up at some ungodly hour because of noise, whatever that noise may be. If you have lodged a complaint during the night, don't forget to ask about getting some sort of discount or other compensation for your disruption.

Be sure and do your research before you book your hotel. If one of your friends or relatives actually works for a hotel, inquire if they can use their discount to book you a room! Just like I have a few friends who are flight attendants and they are able to get me some great deals on airfares; it's called "You scratch my back and I'll scratch yours!"

If you ever fly on "stand by" and the flight is overbooked, you can go to the office of "Airport Accommodations" (also known as "Traveler's Aid Office" usually found in the International Terminal departure area) and get a travel voucher, which will allow you to stay in a four-star hotel for one night for $35.00. If you have a regular ticket and get bumped, you can get a voucher to stay for free.

ABOUT THE AUTHOR

Christie Smith

I have been living in the Southern California desert community of Barstow since December of 2012. My family has a home on twenty acres of land where I enjoy my life with my Thoroughbred horse named Filly, ten chickens, and various cats and dogs. I was born in Los Angeles, California, in 1967 but moved periodically. Growing up, I lived in Poway, CA; Ridgecrest, CA; Honolulu, HI; Reno, NV; Fort Worth, TX; and Everett, WA.

In the early 90's, I traveled to Europe and visited nine countries. As a result, I penned a little travel guide of my experiences (yet to be published).

I grew up keeping diaries and sketching cartoon characters for fun. I was mostly a shy kid, but I had my moments. I had many good friends, some of whom are still my friends now forty years later. I did all the usual stuff growing up: Girl Scouts, Softball, and I even had a case of chickenpox.

I struggled in school because my family moved a lot, and at sixteen years old I was a high-school dropout. I later went back to Adult Education at twenty-two years old and completed my high school diploma. It was a great feeling also because I had a couple of really hard-nosed but caring teachers named Patricia Davis and Millicent Steendal who taught me to love English and who inspired me to write my stories.

For upwards of twenty years, I have worked mostly in high-end four-star hotels that have 500 to over 1,000 rooms; and because I worked the graveyard shift, the stories and shenanigans abound.

I have two grown children who live and work in the Los Angeles area. They are my "Rocks," my best friends, and my confidants. Everything that I've accomplished in life I owe to them; they are my reason for living, surviving, and overcoming the many obstacles that have presented themselves throughout my life. I live by the mottos:

"Don't take life so serious, you'll never get out alive."

and

"I refuse to have a battle of wits with an unarmed person."

Made in the USA
Las Vegas, NV
17 February 2024

85932511R00090